DATE DUE			

JOHN D.
ROCKEFELLER

Empire Builder

JOHN D.
ROCKEFELLER

Empire Builder

By

Ellen Greenman Coffey

❊

THE AMERICAN DREAM

SILVER BURDETT PRESS
ENGLEWOOD CLIFFS, NEW JERSEY

Designed and produced by Blackbirch Graphics, Inc.

Project Editor: Nancy Furstinger

Manufactured in the United States of America

(Lib. ed.) 10 9 8 7 6 5 4 3 2 1

(Paper ed.) 10 9 8 7 6 5 4 3 2 1

Library of Congress Cataloging-in-Publication Data

Coffey, Ellen Greenman.
    John D. Rockefeller / by Ellen Greenman Coffey
    (The American dream series)
    Bibliography: p. 108
    Includes index
    Summary: A biography of the industrialist who made a fortune in the oil business and later became a famous philanthropist, establishing the Rockefeller Foundation in 1913.
    1. Rockefeller, John D. (John Davison), 1839–1937—Juvenile literature.   2. Capitalists and Financiers—United States—Biography—Juvenile literature.   3. Philanthropists—United States—Biography—Juvenile literature.   [1. Rockefeller, John D. (John Davison), 1839–1937.   2. Businessmen.   3. Millionaires.   4. Philanthropists.]   I. Title.   II. Series: American dream (Englewood Cliffs, N.J.)
    HC102.5.R548C34   1989
    338.7'6223382'0924—dc19
    [B]
    [92]   89-4308
                                          CIP
                                          AC

ISBN 0-382-09583-9 (lib. bdg.)
ISBN 0-382-09590-1 (pbk.)

Contents

John D. Rockefeller, right, his sister Mary Ann, and his brother William sat for a daguerrotype in the early 1850s.

Chapter 1

A Boyhood of Business Lessons

*J*ohn Davison Rockefeller, according to his own reminiscences, started his business career at the age of seven. He discovered a wild turkey's nest in the woods near his home in upstate New York. He reported the find to his mother and she encouraged the boy to watch the nest closely. When the eggs hatched, he monitored the young turkeys until they were large enough to be brought home and fattened up for market.

The profits from his first poultry sale were kept in a blue china jar which his mother set aside for that purpose. At her suggestion, he gave a portion of his earnings to the Baptist church the family attended. The rest he saved.

The turkey money wasn't his only income. He had four brothers and sisters to whom he sold candy that he had bought cheaply by the pound. They had to pay him the retail price each time they wanted a piece. He also hired himself out to a neighboring farmer as a day laborer. For ten hours at a stretch, he hoed potatoes in the hot sun and received $.34 for his work. By the time he was ten years old, he had more than $50 put aside. In 1849, when the average weekly wage was less than $5, that was a pretty princely sum for a youngster to have saved.

It was about this time that John D. Rockefeller learned an important lesson about personal finance. The farmer for whom he worked asked to borrow $50. He agreed to pay young John seven percent interest on a year's loan. When it was repaid in full, John realized that the money had earned him as much in interest–$3.50–as he would have made working in the potato fields for more than ten days.

✳

"I cheat my boys every chance I get," he always said. "I want to make 'em sharp."

It certainly seemed to the serious young Rockefeller that letting money work for you was far more rewarding than physical farm labor. Besides, he felt that working out the deal with the farmer had been a satisfying adult thing to do. It was as if he had won at a grown-up's game.

John learned such matters from his father. William Avery Rockefeller was a large, energetic man who came from a line of sober German farmers. His forebears had emigrated to New York State a century before. "Big Bill" Rockefeller, as he was called, was not like his hardworking, straitlaced relatives. He found life on the farm too tedious for his tastes.

He liked meeting new people, swapping tall tales, and cooking up schemes for making money. He was a glib talker and a sharp trader and he wanted his children to be as savvy about business as he was. He taught them some lessons the hard way.

"I cheat my boys every chance I get," he always said. "I want to make 'em sharp. I trade with the boys and I just beat them to be sharp traders."

It was Big Bill who taught young John how to draw up a note for lending money and who instilled in him the idea that a business deal, once made, was a sacred contract. He was to test his son on this principle in later years by calling in loans at very difficult times. Even the dutiful John found these particular trials a bit wearing on occasion.

Big Bill set his family up in a series of farmhouses, but he made his living on the road. As a child John had no idea what his father did as a profession. Big Bill always seemed to have a large wad of bills in his pocket when he was around. When he went away again, he stashed money in the house for his wife to use. Big Bill didn't trust banks.

Sometimes the money he left was enough for the family's needs. But often he was gone for months at a time and John's mother had to struggle to feed and clothe her children. She seemed to have been up to the challenge. A stern and devout Baptist, she possessed none of Big Bill's charm or high spirits. She took her maternal obligations seriously and held her children to high standards for morality and duty.

As the oldest son, John took on many household tasks in his father's absence. Whether his nature made him solemn about his duties or his early responsibilities created his serious approach to life is hard to know. He was, however, a most conscientious and rather humorless boy.

In that respect he was more like his mother than his father. He even looked like her. She was slight and pale and had delicate features. Her one colorful trait was a head of flaming red hair. She had been born Eliza Davison, the daughter of a prosperous New York State farmer whose ancestors came to New England from Scotland. She was in her early twenties when Big Bill Rockefeller came to her family's door to sell patent medicine.

She was taken with him immediately. His vitality, humor, and spontaneity completely captivated this young woman who was so different from him in every way. He wore brocaded vests and a diamond stickpin. She wore high-necked dark dresses that were more practical than fashionable. He talked in hyperbole–exaggerating his stories of how brave or clever he had been. She spoke in adages—well-worn sayings about good behavior, such as "willful waste makes woeful want."

Eliza taught Sunday school and did not approve of alcoholic beverages. Big Bill didn't go to church and, although he didn't drink, he loved the camaraderie of taverns. Eliza, however, did have one vice that Big Bill could never condone and she could never give up. She smoked a corncob pipe.

One account of their first meeting suggests that Big Bill had used one of his favorite selling tricks when he knocked on the Davison's door. He pretended to be deaf and dumb so that people would feel sorry for him and want to buy his product to help him out. He would pull out a slate and a piece of chalk to communicate.

Eliza is reported to have said to her family, "If that man weren't handicapped, I'd marry him." The courtship was short. Eliza Davison married William Avery Rockefeller on February 26, 1837. Big Bill settled his wife into a rented cottage outside Richford, New York, between Binghampton and Ithaca. The house was modest, but it was ringed with apple trees and had a beautiful view of the rolling hills of western New York. Their first three children were born there—Lucy, John, and William. John Davison Rockefeller was born on July 8, 1839.

He was named for his grandfather Davison, whom his mother adored, and was often called John D. at home. Eliza, in truth, missed her family when her husband was on the road. So in 1843, Big Bill bought a farm for Eliza and the children near Moravia, New York, where the Davisons lived. The white clapboard house had seven rooms and a view of Lake Owasco. Although the property included ninety-two acres of land, Big Bill still had no intention of becoming a full-time farmer.

The family did, however, keep cows for their own needs and Big Bill took great pleasure in teaching John D. how to milk them. He also taught the boy

how to handle a team of horses properly and how to hunt. He seemed devoted to the family when he was home.

The children loved having their father home. He brought excitement and fun into their lives. He seemed to revel in their company. He taught them to swim. He played the fiddle for them and taught them songs. He exuded energy and good humor and confidence. They considered him the most worldly and wonderful man alive.

John D., who credited his father with giving him an appreciation for business as an honorable calling, was a rich and successful businessman himself before he was forced to confront some of his father's failings. Even then he kept in touch with Big Bill, and Big Bill was always a welcome guest at John D.'s home.

John D.'s children and grandchildren were to look forward to those visits just as eagerly as John D.

did as a boy. Perhaps Eliza's lifelong affection for Big Bill–the great passion of her life–allowed her son to see him only as the wonderful teacher and patron of his youth.

Big Bill was a flimflam man. He sold patent medicines–usually concoctions that included some form of morphine–as cancer cures to a gullible public. Using false credentials and making outrageous promises for his formulas, he would sell a bottle for as much as $25 to people who hardly made that much money in three months. He first called himself Dr. Rockefeller and later took on a whole separate life as Dr. William Levingston.

In addition to selling quack medicines, Big Bill dabbled in real estate and horse trading all through the Midwest. In 1849, he was accused of rape in Cayuga county, where his family lived. He was never convicted, but his reputation as a womanizer was such that he thought it wisest to move the family out of the county to Oswego.

John D. evidently was told that the new town had better schools for the Rockefeller children, who now numbered five. Mary Ann and a set of twins, Francis and Franklin, had been born in Moravia. Francis died as an infant.

John D. did attend Oswego Academy for one year, but he was not happy there. He later described his grammar teacher as being very harsh and inclined to throw things at the students. John D. also had to work hard to keep up with the work and never felt comfortable in the classroom.

He must have welcomed Big Bill's decision to move the family again in 1853. Eliza did not make her feelings known. But since she had already been away from the Davisons for four years, it probably didn't matter as much. Living in a rural location with five small children was a busy, full life–however lonesome it might be for her. The family had long ago turned inward and found its security and support at home, waiting for Big Bill.

This time they settled about thirteen miles outside Cleveland, Ohio. John D. assumed that his father thought there was more opportunity for his boys near a big city than in rural New York.

Big Bill, who was starting out on one of his most daring and shocking deceptions, probably wanted his family a little farther away from the scene of his double-dealing. That same year he had started courting a young Canadian woman named Margaret Allen. She lived in a small town in Ontario, right over the New York border.

He was forty-three and she was in her late teens when this romance began. She had no idea that her charming Dr. William Levingston had another name and another family. She, like Eliza before her, found life around him so exciting and so stimulating that she could forgive his long absences while he was on the road.

This was not a whirlwind affair. It was two years before Big Bill—still married to Eliza and very involved with his children—wed for the second time. Margaret Allen was twenty and certainly did not suspect that her new husband was a bigamist.

Nor did her family sense anything wrong. They put the couple up for several years before Big Bill took Margaret to Philadelphia to live.

The Levingstons never had children, and Big Bill's double life was not known in John D.'s family until many years later. By then it was accepted that he had made a life for himself in the West, but family letters show no knowledge of another wife. They do show a gentle regard between Eliza and Big Bill—despite the long separations—until her death in 1889.

As much as he admired and looked up to his father, John D. was his mother's son. It was she who truly influenced him with her day-to-day caring and example. And that is probably why he never turned on his father when he finally was faced with the old man's double life.

His mother forgave Big Bill. So would he.

Cleveland, Ohio, was a major port on Lake Erie, where produce was shipped from the Middle West to Buffalo, New York, and the Erie Canal.

Taking on Cleveland

*T*he Rockefellers had no sooner set up housekeeping in their new home when Big Bill decided it was time that John D. got a taste of city life. Girls, he felt, could be educated at home. But his oldest boy needed to know about the world and Cleveland seemed a pretty good place to start.

The year was 1853. Cleveland already had a population of more than 25,000. Two years earlier the railroad from the East had reached the city, giving competition to the Erie Canal. This man-made waterway allowed ships from such Lake Erie ports as Cleveland to continue to navigate from Buffalo, New York, to the Hudson River at Albany, New York, and on down the Hudson to the Atlantic Ocean at New York City. Opened in 1825, the Erie Canal made Ohio ports like Cleveland very important hubs of commerce, particularly for agricultural products.

In 1827 another canal was opened that connected Cleveland with the Ohio River, the principal shipping route to the western part of the United States. This made Cleveland one of the major crossroads for all the traffic from the eastern seaboard to the rest of the country. Products from all around Lake Erie could now be shipped westward as easily as they could be shipped eastward.

The Cleveland waterfront was alive with activity in the early 1850s when John D. first saw it. He loved to stand along the lakefront and watch the loading and unloading of schooners full of grain and other farm produce from the Midwest and side-wheelers full of manufactured goods from the East Coast. Watching the waterway activity became an education as well as his principal entertainment.

However, it was for a more conventional education that his father had brought him to Cleveland. Big Bill found the young man a room in a boardinghouse and enrolled him in Central High School. With that accomplished, Big Bill returned to the road and John D. was left on his own. He was fourteen years old.

John D. was serious about school, but he did not find it easy. He liked math because he was good at figures, and calculations interested him. His other subjects were more difficult. He had little background in literature or the sciences to rely upon.

Nor did he have any social graces to help him. He had lived his entire life, except for the one unhappy year at the Oswego Academy, surrounded almost exclusively by his family. The other young people he knew were all farmers' children, like himself. He had not inherited his father's gift for friendly banter. Rather, he was shy and introspective, like his mother.

The other students at Central High School came mostly from wealthy families. In those days, only the well-to-do could afford to let a teenage child go to high school rather than to work. John D. was much more ambitious than his fellow students, but he had to struggle harder than many of them to keep up with his lessons. He was truly a country bumpkin among the city slickers.

There were two fellow students the young John D. did take an interest in. He would become closer to them later, when he had gained more confidence in himself. One was a young man named Marcus Alonzo Hanna, who would go on to college before entering Cleveland's business world and making his fortune.

Mark Hanna, like John D., was to ride the post-Civil War industrial boom in Ohio to considerable riches. Unlike John D., he then took an avid interest in politics and was responsible for the election of Ohio's William McKinley to the governorship of the state and later to the presidency of the United States.

The other student John D. noticed was Laura Celestia Spelman, a spirited and pretty young woman whose high-school commencement speech advocated women's independence. She also would go on to college while John D. began to establish himself in business. But he did not forget her. She eventually became his wife.

John D. found solace and a social life during his high-school years at the Erie Street Baptist Church. He attended services twice on Sunday and prayer meetings on Friday nights. Within a year he had been baptized.

The church membership was made up essentially of working-class families, and John D. felt comfortable with them. These clerks, shopkeepers, and artisans were more like the farmers he was accustomed to than the other students at the high school. He attended all the church suppers and social meetings he could, and the congregation made him feel welcome and part of the group.

His loyalty to this small church that harbored him when he was new to the city and lonely would make the Baptists one of the wealthiest denomina-

Taking on Cleveland

William Avery Rockefeller (1810–1909), John D.'s father.

tions in the United States before the turn of the century.

Besides his reputation as a math whiz, John D. earned considerable respect as a clear thinker in high-school debates. He was neither passionate nor dramatic, but his quiet, patient presentation of his side was always precise and well-organized.

John D. finished high school in 1855. He did not bother to attend the graduation ceremonies or to pick up his diploma. He made no effort to apply for a traditional college degree, but he did sign up for a series of accounting and bookkeeping courses at Folsom Commercial College. His tuition was $40 and seems to have been well worth it to him.

He later wrote of how exciting he found the experience of learning the secrets of keeping balance sheets. To him it was fascinating to be able "to know at all times the resources and the liabilities, to keep an exact record of just how business stood."

When his business courses were over, John D. went home for a month's vacation with his mother and sisters and brothers. His younger brother William was particularly eager to hear about life in Cleveland. He was scheduled to enter Central High School the next year.

Big Bill was not at home and certainly none of the family could have guessed that he was honeymooning with a new bride, whom he had married on June 12. Nor did Big Bill join the family to celebrate John D.'s sixteenth birthday on July 8.

The graduate returned to Cleveland in mid-August to begin his career. He was determined that he would not settle for an errand boy's job. He wanted a position in which he could learn something and make a contribution. "I did not guess what it would be, but I was after something big," he later wrote about his first venture into the business world.

Eliza Davison Rockefeller (1814–1889), John D.'s mother.

He had no important friends in Cleveland nor any letters of introduction to businessmen. What he did have was tireless energy and a sense of mission. He obtained a city directory. From it he made a list of prominent and prosperous companies for whom he thought he might like to work.

Each morning he got up early, bathed and dressed carefully in his best suit, ate a simple breakfast, and set out on his rounds. At each bank, shipping firm, or railroad office that he entered, he asked to speak to the man in charge. If he didn't get the top person, which was the usual case, he would try his

A typical nineteenth century office featured a tall desk for the bookkeepers, and was dominated by an enormous coal- or wood-burning stove.

carefully prepared speech on the best substitute he could get to listen.

He was offering energy and dedication for a chance to learn the business. With no working experience nor references, he was no different from any other young man looking for a job. Unfortunately, Cleveland was full of such young men, attracted by the hustle and deal-making of a fast-growing port city.

John D. made the rounds from early morning until closing time six days a week. At night he would study his list, make notes, and figure out the next day's route. When he had called once on each establishment on his list, he simply started over and began making second calls. He never stooped to adding smaller or less prestigious firms to the list.

Weeks went by with no offers. John D. may have been discouraged, but he didn't stop his rounds. Nor did he ever consider taking a stopgap job as a clerk or a messenger. He knew what he wanted and he had the persistence to keep after it.

Finally Big Bill came to see him. He saw how difficult it was to find work in Cleveland and suggested that John D. go back to the country for a while. "I'll take care of you," his father told him. But John D. did not want to remain dependent on his father. The thought of returning home defeated made him feel "a cold chill down my spine," he later wrote.

He kept to his methodical calls on all the companies on his list. He kept his suit clean and pressed, and he kept to his day-long schedule from Monday through Saturday. He simply refused to believe that his persistence would not pay off eventually.

John D. was right. Toward the end of September, he made a second call on a commission house called Hewitt and Tuttle. He was interviewed by Henry B. Tuttle, the junior partner in the company. Tuttle was in charge of the books and needed help.

"Come back after dinner," he told John D. The senior partner, Isaac L. Hewitt, would be able to meet him then. If Hewitt agreed, they might hire him for a three-month trial as a bookkeeper.

John D. later said that he maintained his dignity along the block where Hewitt and Tuttle was located. But, as soon as he turned the corner, he started to skip with joy and skipped all the way back to the boardinghouse. He scarcely touched his dinner.

Hewitt was more interested in John D.'s handwriting than in his enthusiasm, and the samples that the young man produced seemed to pass muster. He was told to report to work the next morning.

Not a word was said about salary, but John D. didn't care. He figured he could manage with almost any amount. His room cost one dollar a week and he didn't eat very much. What was important was that he had his foot in the door. That was all that he asked. The rest, he knew, was up to him.

The date was September 26, 1855. To John D. it was the most significant date in his career. It was the beginning of his life as a businessman. And he was to commemorate this anniversary ever afterward as if it were his birthday and the Fourth of July all rolled up into one.

No matter where he and his family were, on September 26, the American flag would be raised over the house and dinner would be a celebration feast.

John D. Rockefeller in 1857, two years before he opened his own firm at the age of twenty.

Chapter 3

The Career Man
at Sixteen

*J*ohn D. Rockefeller's first job was that of a bookkeeper-clerk, not unlike the position Bob Cratchit held with Scrooge. And his tools were certainly the same—a dip pen and ledger and a blotter. Fountain pens had not yet come into use in 1855.

To keep careful, legible books took patience and skillful, attentive penmanship. Copies of bills of lading and contracts had to be made by hand as well. There was no carbon paper to speed things along.

Such tasks were not laborious to the young graduate of accounting school. To him it was thrilling to compile numbers that represented real shipments, real prices, and real commissions.

Hewitt and Tuttle was a commission house. The two partners were the middlemen who put buyers and sellers together and arranged shipment and payment, all for a percentage or commission. In a city like Cleveland, which was surrounded by farming states, the major products being bought and sold were agricultural produce. But commission houses also dealt in building materials such as lumber and marble and anything else that might be shipped.

And not all the commission-house business was done on commission. Often a company like Hewitt and Tuttle would buy an entire shipment of grain outright from a farmer. The company would then sell the whole crop to a wholesaler in the East and arrange for its storage and transportation via the most economical route.

Commission houses had to be shrewd to make money in these deals because prices could fluctuate quickly. If a commission house bought too high, it might have to unload at a loss. The telegraph kept such companies apprised of prices and market conditions around the country, so they could make educated guesses about the best time to buy and sell and what to pay. Smart traders had to keep up and move swiftly when they saw a good opportunity.

John D. worked long hours over the Hewitt and Tuttle books. He arose early and opened the office at 6:30 a.m. and stayed until dinner time. He often came back after his meal and put in several more hours by the light of the whale-oil lamp on his high desk. For his three-month trial period he was paid $16 a month. He didn't mind. This was his apprenticeship and he was learning the ways of the commission business as thoroughly as anyone could.

The bills he checked and the accounts he kept were not dry, meaningless figures to be recorded. They were the inside story of a genuine business and how it was run. John D. checked and double-checked everything that passed through his desk. Then he went home at night and reviewed the day's activities to see where things might have been done more economically or efficiently.

He pored over old ledgers in the office as well. To him they told the history of the commission-house business and he wanted to know it all. He was not a word person, but numbers could sing to him.

In fact, his own diary was a ledger book started when he returned to Cleveland to find work. He made daily entries about the money he had spent and the money he had received. Every penny was accounted for, and these figures told the story of his adult life.

When his three months were up, Hewitt and Tuttle raised his salary to $31 a month and began involving John D. in more aspects of the business. He was a happy young man. He found the methods and systems of bookkeeping "delightful," and he felt that he was in a "gentleman's position" even though he was still only sixteen years old. He liked the fact that men along the waterfront addressed him as Mr. Rockefeller.

His life six days a week revolved solely around the commission house. But his ledger shows that he still attended the Erie Street Baptist Church regularly and gave at least ten percent of his salary to its different committees and projects. This tithing to the church may not have been very impressive when he was making less than $4 a week, but it was a practice he continued even when he was called "the richest man in America" not too many years later.

Mr. Tuttle retired from business before John D. had finished his first year with the firm. The young man took over many of the former partner's duties, and his salary was raised to $50 a month. Working side by side with Mr. Hewitt, John D. posted the books, handled all the cash, wrote all the checks, and paid all the bills.

He took his responsibilities very seriously. "I scrutinized every bill. If it had ever so many items, I went over each one, verified it, and carefully added the totals. The bill had to be accurate in every detail before I okayed it to be paid," he later wrote.

And he stood his ground when he was challenged. A schooner captain is said to have grown

✳

His favorite Bible text was "Seest thou a man diligent in business? He shall stand before kings."

quite irate with the young accountant for holding up a check for his cargo.

John D. insisted that the amount of the captain's bill did not tally with the actual cargo received. The captain said he shouldn't worry about it, that everybody allowed for a margin of error.

Everybody but John D. The young man told the captain that if he didn't make his bill match the weight and price of his cargo, then the next time the captain himself wouldn't trust John D. or his firm.

"If I am going to do right by you, I can't begin by cheating somebody else, can I? If I did, you would soon be afraid that I would cheat you, too. Isn't that so?" he asked the schooner captain.

How the captain felt is not recorded. But he got a check for the amount John D. thought he was due. This accuracy in bookkeeping was a business principle that John D. would never relinquish.

In his new capacity, John D. spent a considerable amount of his time dealing with railroad freight agents, schooner captains, and canal barge owners. He was becoming an expert on the ins and outs of the transportation business. This was crucial for a commission house because freight costs could eat up profits in a hurry.

John D. learned to negotiate settlements for late or damaged shipments with as many as three separate carriers for a single load. And he came to realize that posted rates–which he had thought were a standard for everyone, big and small–also could be negotiated. Favored customers, he discovered, were billed by the standard rates but then received a rebate at the end of the month.

This was a serious study period, and John D. happily devoted all his waking hours to the commission house. His one diversion was church, where he taught Sunday school with a businesslike confidence. His favorite Bible text was "Seest thou a man diligent in business? He shall stand before kings."

He felt then that his own diligence was blessed and he never questioned his own morality in business later.

By 1857 John D. had become conversant enough in the commission-house business to realize that Hewitt was not an effective entrepreneur. The country suffered a depression that year and the firm almost went under. Hewitt had his money tied up in warehouses and land deals, along with legal fees brought on by his habit of using the courts frequently to settle problems.

John D. had his first experiences collecting bad debts owed the firm. He had seen Big Bill successfully confront Hewitt about repayment of a loan, but he knew he simply didn't have the powerful presence of his robust father with the silver tongue.

He used a quieter, more persistent method that was to become his hallmark in business. He never raised his voice nor lost his temper. But he also never gave up. Using a calm, unemotional tone, he wore his adversaries down. He believed that he was right and that eventually his opponent would understand that and respond accordingly.

He was gaining a confidence in his own abilities and this was beginning to make him restless.

By this time Big Bill had himself listed in the Cleveland directory as a "botanic physician." He was beginning to work even the Cleveland area with his signs that read:

Dr. William A. Rockefeller
The Celebrated Cancer Specialist
Here for One Day Only
All Cases of Cancer Cured
Unless Too Far Gone and They Can
Be Greatly Benefited

Big Bill had seen two of his sons through high school–William followed John D. at Central High–and also had a second wife to support. He saw the frontier of the country moving westward and he wanted to go with it. That's where his brand of wheeling and dealing was most successful.

He decided it was time to bring Eliza and the girls to Cleveland, where William and John D. could look after them. With that in mind, he bought property on Cheshire Street and set aside money for a house to be built. He put this project in John D.'s hands and promptly left town.

As a boy, John D. had been put in charge of buying firewood. Big Bill berated him badly if he found his son had accepted any green wood or rotted logs in the cord that he had bought. John D. wasn't going to be caught short this time in Big Bill's eyes.

Perhaps the contractor who gave the nineteen-year-old the low bid for the house thought he could cut corners because he was dealing with an inexperienced kid. Before the project was finished, even John D.'s sister Mary Ann felt sorry for the man. She admitted it was the contractor's own fault for bidding so low, but she was sure he lost money on the job.

John D., with his usual perseverance and attention to detail, supervised every nail that went into the house and had the contractor account for every penny. It was a splendid house for the money.

When Hewitt offered to raise John D.'s salary to $700 a year in late 1858, John D. said he thought he deserved $800. He was, after all, doing all of Tuttle's work and more. Hewitt said he would think about it.

Hewitt underestimated the determination of his young employee. He let weeks go by without addressing the issue and seemed not to have worried much about it.

John D. was approached by an acquaintance from the Folsom Commercial College who had also been working as a clerk at a commission house. His name was Maurice B. Clark and he had immigrated to the United States from England. He was twenty-eight years old and had saved $2,000.

Clark suggested that if John D. also could come up with $2,000, they could go into partnership and start their own commission house. John D. had saved $800 from his salary and a few side speculations. The proposition interested John D. and he started looking around for guidance and financial help.

"I talked the matter over with my father," he wrote later. "He told me he had always intended to give each of his children $1,000 when they reached twenty-one." There was a hitch, of course. John D. was still nineteen. Big Bill, still the tough trader with his children, offered to advance John D. the money at ten percent interest until he reached his twenty-first birthday.

"I accepted gladly my father's offer," he wrote.

John D.—having never heard another word from Hewitt about the raise he had asked for—quietly left the firm in April 1859 to start his own commission house with Clark.

Hewitt and Tuttle went under within the year.

John D. supervised the building of the Rockefeller house at 33 Cheshire Street in Cleveland, Ohio.

In the nineteenth century, before the invention of the typewriter and adding machine, bookkeeping and secretarial work were done by hand, and women were not yet part of the office workforce.

Partnerships and Prosperity

*T*he new commission house of Clark and Rockefeller opened its doors in April 1859. Although Clark, by seniority, gave himself first billing in the title, it was Rockefeller who truly ran the firm.

Or so he liked to remember it many years later. From the beginning, he was the office person who kept the books and negotiated the logistics of moving shipments of produce and goods. Clark worked outside the office, traveling the countryside to obtain consignments from farmers.

There was considerable competition among commission houses, so Clark and Rockefeller advertised themselves as offering more liberal advances on crops than other commission houses. These advances were important to farmers who needed the money to pay off their loans for seed and equipment. For more cash up front, they would sell their crops for less.

However, it meant that Clark and Rockefeller had to put out a lot of money before they sold their consignments and got paid themselves. If prices should fall in the meantime, they could lose their profit margin and possibly even some of their buying price. It also meant that they had to negotiate warehouse space and transportation costs very carefully to protect their share of the sale price.

John D. had learned from Big Bill the importance of borrowing when you needed cash to get in on a good deal. In fact, he started out by borrowing from his father—always at ten percent interest. But soon he needed even greater sums.

He began cultivating the banks in Cleveland. He had certainly earned a reputation for carefulness and integrity while working for Hewitt and Tuttle, but he also was only nineteen years old. He went first to the bank where Clark and Rockefeller kept their deposits.

The bank's president was Truman P. Handy. He asked John D. how much he wanted to borrow and never blinked when the young man said $2,000. (The bank's interest rate was less than Big Bill's.) John D. never forgot Handy's early trust in him. Some years later, he offered Handy a chance to buy Standard Oil stock, but Handy did not have enough cash at the time to take advantage of the offer. John D.—out of loyalty to an old friend—lent him the money.

John D. was perhaps so grateful to Handy because the other bankers were not all so gracious. They were suspicious of such a young man wanting to borrow what, in those days, were hefty sums of money for purposes that the bankers considered to be speculative.

John D. was not easily put off. He hounded the bank presidents in much the same way he had chased the people who owed money to Hewitt and Tuttle. He was calm, polite, and persistent.

"What if a president of a bank refused to make me a loan?" he later wrote. "That was nothing. He might lecture me on the folly of making a loan for the purpose for which I was seeking it. That made no difference to me; it simply meant I must look elsewhere until I got what I wanted." He did always look elsewhere until he found the money he needed.

Their first year in business, Clark and Rockefeller did nearly $500,000 in trading, netting the partners $4,400. The returns were not bad for a new business with start-up expenses. And for a young man who had the year before earned $600, it was a sizable jump in income. By the second year–1860–they netted $17,000.

John D. was just as persistent in getting the railroad cars and ship space he needed to move his consignments. He wrote of his own activities in lining up transportation. According to him, he just kept "pegging away at the railroad companies with the greatest urgency, and there were times I well remember when they manifested their displeasure at our persistency in no uncertain terms."

But it was not John D.'s persistency that Clark objected to; it was the enormous amount of loan money to which he signed their names. To Clark, John D. was "the greatest borrower I ever saw." He was nine years older than John D. and had seen a good deal more of business. To him the business was a comfortable and secure living, not a mission.

Unlike his partner, Clark was not driven to become a wealthy man. He was, therefore, less comfortable with the outstanding loans that they might not be able to pay back. He was also more easygoing than John D.

John D. later wrote about Clark's good-natured handling of customers, of which John D. clearly disapproved. It seems a regular client of the firm had come into the office and asked Clark for an advance on a shipment of produce for which there was no bill of lading. Clark, recognizing the man and appreciating his need for the money, assured him he would have a check by the end of the day.

Rockefeller found out what had happened and refused to go along with the advance. Clark left the office in a fury. When the customer returned, John D. confronted him with a firm policy of no advance before a bill of lading was in hand. The customer stormed out of the office after a heated exchange.

Rockefeller–always sure he was right–said the incident actually helped Clark and Rockefeller. The client, as it turned out, had been sent by a country bank to test the company's responsibility before approving a loan. They got the loan and did not lose their old customer–who came back laughing–after all.

While Rockefeller was freely speculating with the company's money, he was more cautious with his own extra funds. He still gave generously to the church, and, since he was living with his family in the new Cleveland house, he also invested privately in land and railroad stock.

Rockefeller's sense of rivalry with his partner drove him to try his own hand at working the farmlands for consignments, the job normally handled by Clark. John D. traveled through rural Ohio and Indiana and claims to have been very successful at attracting new customers.

While the uneasy partners were managing the commission-house business in spite of their differences, another entrepreneur was pioneering a new business in northwest Pennsylvania. In 1859, E.L. Drake drilled the first producing oil well near a stream called Oil Creek because of the black ooze it often contained. The site shortly thereafter became know as Titusville.

This crude oil, or petroleum, was not a new substance. It appeared in streams such as Oil Creek or bubbled to the surface in small holes where people could scoop it up in small quantities. It had been used through the centuries as mortar in walls and boat hulls. The Indians of North America used it in medicine–which was sold to the early settlers under the name "Seneca oil"–and as an ingredient in paint. This crude oil was a part of Big Bill's patent medicines.

Petroleum became important at the time of Drake's dramatic exploit because scientists had found that crude oil could be easily and cheaply refined into kerosene for lamps. In the middle of the nineteenth century, light in homes and businesses in America was provided by candles and whale-oil lamps. Candles were messy, dangerous, and expensive. They burned down too quickly. Whale-oil lamps gave more illumination for the money, but they also gave off an unpleasant smell and a dirty, sooty smoke.

Kerosene made from coal was a great improvement. It burned slowly and cleanly. It had been produced in Europe in the early part of the nineteenth century. In fact, in 1815 several streets in Prague, the capital city of Czechoslovakia, were lighted with kerosene lamps.

When Drake probed and found a major deposit of oil that he was able to bring out of the earth, it was exciting and attractive to speculators because it meant a cheap source of kerosene to light the lamps of the world.

The internal combustion engine had not yet evolved beyond a theory. All the other by-products of petroleum that make up the oil industry today–fuel for vehicles and factories, heating oil and gas, lubricants, drugs, dyes, and synthetics–had no role in the early petroleum boom. Good, cheap light was the only issue.

Drake's oil well brought to northwest Pennsylvania the same notoriety and expectation of quick riches as John Sutter's discovery of gold had brought to California a decade before. Cities like Titusville sprang up almost overnight; land prices soared and people swarmed to the area to make their fortunes.

The Oil Region, as the area became known, was dotted with rickety derricks as more and more wells

The first oil wells
were discovered
in northwestern
Pennsylvania at Titusville
near Oil Creek.

were dug. Burly men drove massive teams of horses through the oil-slicked mud to get the crude oil to the railroads that would take it to refineries, first in Pittsburgh and New York and then in Cleveland.

John D. watched the oil business with interest. In fact, he even visited the Oil Region himself to see what was happening. A meticulous organizer who could envision the big picture in all its detail, he saw no immediate opportunity for himself. He decided that serious profits would not be made at the site of the wells, but in the refining and distribution of the kerosene. This aspect of the business was still chaotic.

The commission house was prospering and Rockefeller decided just to watch the oil business for a while. He and Clark were becoming busier and busier. The details of their enterprise occupied all of John D.'s waking hours from Monday through Saturday.

Sundays were still devoted to the Erie Street Baptist Church, where John D. was now a deacon. He had helped the church pay off its mortgage by buttonholing parishioners after services and applying the same kind of courteous, persistent pressure he used on bank presidents to get them to contribute to the cause.

In April 1861, the U.S. Civil War began. Ohioans, who had never had slaves, were strongly in favor of preserving the Union. There were many abolitionists in the state, and the underground railway that helped slaves escape the South had brought many black people to safety in Ohio.

Volunteers quickly joined up under fellow Ohioan Ulysses S. Grant. Mobilization of the Union Army required supplies in quantities that only a well-organized and detail-oriented company like Clark and Rockefeller could successfully provide. Commodity prices soared and the partnership became more and more proficient in its work and more and more successful in its profits.

John D.'s youngest brother Frank, still only six-teen, wanted to join the Union Army. He was two years too young, but he was determined to go re-gardless. With Eliza's strict morality behind him, he carefully chalked the number 18 on the soles of each of his boots. Then when he was asked his age he could say without technically lying, "I'm over eigh-teen, sir." He was accepted.

Frank got to the front and was wounded twice. John D. followed the events of the war on two large maps in the office and contributed money to the cause–enough, he told his contemporaries, to outfit ten men. In later years, he said that it was twenty or even thirty. "I wanted to go in the Army and do my part," he wrote. "But it was simply out of the ques-tion. There was no one to take my place. We were in a new business, and if I had not stayed it must have stopped–and with so many dependent on it."

Not everyone in Cleveland was as cautious about the new oil business as John D. was. Refineries–which were not expensive to build–were springing up along the railroad route in great numbers. It was almost inevitable that John D. would be approached to participate in the new enterprise.

He had talents the new industry needed. He knew how to move products efficiently from supplier to client, and refiners needed to get the kerosene out quickly and cheaply.

An English friend of Clark's, Samuel Andrews, approached the partners in 1863. A chemist and a mechanic, he had built a superior refinery, but he knew very little about business and he needed help. John D. knew and liked Andrews, who was a mem-ber of the Erie Street Baptist Church, but he was still leery of the oil industry as a long-term enterprise. After all, he and Clark were becoming wealthy from the commission-house business. Why should they change focus now?

However, John D. had extra cash and agreed to become a silent partner in the new company that

Cleveland, Ohio, founded in 1796, grew rapidly after the Ohio-Erie canal was built in 1830. Many of the towns and cities in the Western Reserve were laid out in a grid.

Andrews wanted to form. Andrews' partner was Clark's brother, James, whose job would be to go to the Oil Region and bargain for crude oil. Andrews would run the refinery and John D., who had put $4,000 into the new company, would simply be one

of the investors in Andrews, Clark and Company.

And so, for $4,000 John D. reluctantly entered the oil business. It was not his major concern, though; he was twenty-four years old and his thoughts were turning elsewhere.

Portrait of Laura Spelman Rockefeller.

Courtship and New Commitment

Young John D. Rockefeller may not have inherited his father's robust stature and charismatic personality, but he was an attractive man with his stately posture, enormous energy, and courtly manners. In his early twenties he dressed conservatively but in the modish cut of the day. He sported stylish sideburns when they were in fashion and later a thick reddish-brown moustache and mutton-chop whiskers when they were in vogue.

He was tall and lithe and, for all the soberness of his hard work and churchgoing, he indulged himself in the finest horses he could find to pull his buggy, which he would race with any man at the drop of a hat. He was accustomed to winning in business and he made sure he won in buggy racing as well. He could be downright reckless in a buggy race if the outcome was close. He kept a separate page in his ledger to document all expenses for his horses, who were well taken care of.

John D. had in his youth cultivated the calm, exterior manner that became his hallmark. He never seemed in a hurry, nor did he ever appear impatient. He treated everyone from a favored customer to an office clerk with the same easy courtesy and attention.

He was a good listener and revealed his own feelings very seldom, and then only in the company of coworkers. One business associate once wrote of hearing John D. let out a whoop of delight when one of his buyers cornered a batch of crude oil for a particularly low price. He jumped up and down and even embraced the startled man. Another one caught him gleefully leaping about his office at good news and chanting, "I'm bound to be rich! I'm bound to be rich!" These outbursts of emotion were very rare for the disciplined young man. They would become even rarer as he matured.

One feature betrayed his serene facade. John D.'s penetrating, steely grey-blue eyes gave hints of the tremendous intellectual energy and drive behind the man. He would fix people with his eyes while he talked to them in a quiet, friendly, matter-of-fact tone. They were flattered by his complete concentration and disarmed by his gentle speech. It was *his* unique kind of charm—so different from his father's—but every bit as effective. Some opponents found the eyes to be very cold—chilling, in fact—however, no one failed to notice them.

By the time he was twenty-four, John D. was one of the most successful and respected businessmen in Cleveland. He finally felt secure enough and confident enough to start a family of his own. He would surely have been considered one of the most eligible bachelors in Cleveland.

Although his social life had continued to be confined to church meetings, no woman at Erie Street Baptist Church had caught his fancy. The years had not changed his initial good impressions of the young woman in his high-school class who had been so outspoken about female independence.

Laura Celestia Spelman had gone from Central High School to Oread Collegiate Institute in Worcester, Massachusetts, where she had been editor of the college paper. She had covered lectures by Ralph Waldo Emerson, the poet and transcendental thinker, and by John Brown, the abolitionist.

She returned to Cleveland to teach. Her interest in Christian living was matched only by her commitment to improve the lot of American blacks, a commitment that had only grown stronger in college. Her father, a successful businessman in Cleveland and an Ohio state legislator, was very active on the underground railroad that helped black slaves escape from the South before the Civil War.

Both father and daughter continued to be concerned about the welfare of Afro-Americans during and after the war. They also shared a belief in evils of alcohol and were active in the temperance movement.

John D. did not seem in the least put off by a young woman who could and did think for herself. In fact, he was attracted by her high moral principles and commitment. She was also an attractive woman, with deep, wide-set eyes and thick, dark hair, which she wore parted in the middle and held back in a bun.

The courtship is documented in his ledger. For a number of weeks, there is a $.50 entry under "sundry expenses" for flowers. There is a hansom cab rental of $1.75 for taking Cettie, as he called her, and a chaperone to the Rocky River for an outing. Then there is $15.75 for a ring.

The couple was married at 2 p.m. on September 8, 1864, in the Spelman house.

Cettie joined the Erie Street Baptist Church, where she, too, conducted a Sunday school class. She retired from her teaching job to run the roomy house on Euclid Avenue which John D. bought for them. Unusual for a man of his time, John D. saw his

✳

"Her judgment was always better than mine. Without her keen advice I would be a poor man."

The Erie Canal, which opened in 1825, brought settlers to the west, and shipped produce east to the Hudson River and the port of New York.

marriage as a partnership. He respected and trusted Cettie's views and consulted her about all his business dealings.

For many years, he had her read all his business letters and correct the spelling, which was his weak point. Later he had a secretary to do that, but he still solicited his wife's opinion about what he was writing. "Her judgment was always better than mine," he was to write of her later. "Without her keen advice I would be a poor man."

With his life partner chosen and won, John D. was able to take a harder look at his business part-

ners. Maurice Clark's timidity about financing the
expansion of their company and his brother Jim
Clark's gambling approach to oil buying made John
D. very uncomfortable. He was willing to take risks,
but only after careful study and calculation. He disapproved of gambling as a recreation, and he certainly did not condone it in business.

He had slowly but steadily become a very active
silent partner in Andrews, Clark and Company, and
he was beginning to see more of a future in oil than
in the commission house. The war was winding
down, signaling a cutback in the commission busi-

ness, and more oil wells had been successfully drilled in Pennsylvania to keep up the supply of crude.

John D., the organizer and transportation expert, had picked the site for the company's expanded refinery. This site was right between the new Atlantic and Western railroad tracks, which went straight to the Oil Region, and to the Cayuga River, which gave access to Lake Erie and the Erie Canal for cheap transport to New York in the ice-free months. He saw the strategic advantage in having as many ways of moving crude in and refined kerosene out as possible. It meant one could bargain for better transportation prices and could always make deliveries one way or another.

The more John D. observed the logistics of the oil business, the more he interfered in the company's practices. He had Andrews and Clark build their own cooperage, where barrels were made to store the oil. Buying their own white oak and making their own distinctive blue barrels brought the net cost of a barrel down to 96 cents. To buy from outside sources cost $2.50 per barrel and the products were inferior. They leaked and wasted oil. John D. also put a plumber on staff to save on expensive outside contracts for equipment repairs. He invested in the company's own wagons and horses to keep it from being gouged by the teamsters in the Oil Region.

All of this, of course, cost money and the firm was by now $100,000 in debt to local banks. Tensions in the offices of Clark and Rockefeller and Andrews and Clark built up dramatically. John D. could not understand the Clarks' reluctance to keep expanding. It seemed clear to him that the money they were spending would make them the most efficient and competitive—therefore, the richest—refinery in the country. The Clarks were terrified of not being able to repay the loans.

But in that era, the risks did not seem small. Then $100,000 was more than most people made in a

lifetime, and crude oil prices fluctuated from $20 a barrel to $3 a barrel within a matter of days.

John D., in a weak moment, shared his frustration about the Clark brothers with Andrews. To his surprise, Andrews told him that if there was to be a dissolution of the company, he would stick with Rockefeller.

This was the spur John D. needed. With his usual thoroughness, he covered all the related contingencies first. When he had everything in order, he then could confront the Clarks. He put money into other investments to protect his family. Next, he made the rounds of the Cleveland financial community to see if his personal credit rating was still good. It was, and banks were willing to give him a loan.

Rockefeller and Andrews opened their office in Cleveland, Ohio, in a building with other commission merchants and insurance agents.

Courtship and New Commitment

John D. then backed the Clarks into a corner. When the impasse between the two philosophies of how to run the company became clear and irreconcilable, the Clarks suggested selling. They agreed to auction off the two businesses to the highest bidder. The sale took place on February 2, 1865. John D. represented himself and Andrews. Maurice B. Clark acted for the brothers.

Clark opened the bidding at $500. Rockefeller offered $1,000. The price went up by thousands rapidly. At $60,000, there was some gasping, but neither side was ready to give in. When the price hit $70,000, there was a long silence. Maurice Clark finally broke it by offering $72,000. John D. didn't blink. He immediately countered with $72,500. The Clarks capitulated.

John D. described the moment later as "the day that I determined my career." He said that he felt the bigness of it, but that he had maintained a calmness throughout the proceedings that belied his excitement.

John D. was twenty-six years old and he owned his own business, renamed Rockefeller and Andrews. His company already ran the largest refinery in Cleveland. Its capacity was 500 barrels a day, twice its nearest competitor's. Rockefeller and Andrews brought in revenues of $1 million its first year and twice that the second year.

John D.'s timing was right. He got into the oil business as it was about to start its first big boom, and his instincts for expansion were absolutely correct.

The Clarks, toward whom John D. never was able to mellow, used their $72,500 to start their own refinery. They cannot have been as incompetent as John D. believed them to be, because he would later have to buy them out again when the Clark brothers owned the most prominent competing refinery standing in the way of Rockefeller's Standard Oil Company.

John D. sensed the triumph of his moment and devoted all his considerable energies and passion for detail to mastering the new business. More than two-thirds of the kerosene from Cleveland was destined for foreign markets through New York City. John D. didn't want to entrust this important marketing job to a broker. He persuaded his brother William to join him in the new venture and to go East to represent the company.

William, who had followed John D. through Central High School and into Cleveland's business life, was truly Big Bill's son. He looked like his father and had inherited his father's outgoing, enthusiastic personality. He was a good choice for handling the export trade.

There was no question that John D. was finally onto "something big" as he had always aspired to be. However, as he later explained to a would-be biographer, "None of us ever dreamed of the magnitude of what became of the later expansion."

The expansion of the railroads in the 1850s and 1860s made the shipment of oil from the oil fields to the refineries an easier and cheaper business.

The Pious
Robber Baron

*I*n the Middle Ages in Europe, unscrupulous feudal lords built castles along the narrow passages of the Rhine River so they could control all passing river traffic. To safely pass, travelers and merchants moving goods had to pay heavy tribute to these lords. These "robber barons," as they were known, grew quite wealthy harassing and robbing people traveling through their domain.

The reputation of the robber barons through the ages has not grown sweeter. In the absence of any control from a high authority, they simply leeched their livelihood from the legitimate business activities of other people who had the misfortune to travel through their territory. It finally took more powerful princes and kings to stop them.

When John D. Rockefeller decided that his future lay in the oil business, the industry was in chaos. No one knew when new oil wells would be located and successfully drilled. As a consequence, supplies of oil were very erratic. One week, the railroads couldn't put enough cars into service to move the crude. The next week, the same cars sat idle in the yards.

Oil prices went up and down with the supply, as did prices for the refined kerosene that then had to be delivered to market. Sharp speculators and traders, as well as gamblers and con men and crooks, were in competition all over the Oil Region.

At first, John D. had stayed out of the oil business because he was not convinced that the original oil strikes were not isolated hits that soon would be pumped dry. Only after he saw many new wells struck over several years, did he accept the reality: this dark, viscous substance was in fact a deposit of what many called "black gold."

Once he made a commitment to the industry as his major source of income, John D. saw himself as the appropriate person to bring order to the chaos. He traveled to the Oil Region many times and spoke to everyone in the business who would talk to him, from teamsters and drill operators to refinery owners and railroad executives. In his thorough and methodical way, he was doing his homework. It was the only way he knew or trusted to learn the business.

His first significant decision was that the most reliable and important part of the business was the refining process. The raw material had to be refined in order to be a useful and salable commodity. Here was a part of the business, John D. realized, where a good manager could compete against his rivals by using better technology and more economical handling of storage and shipping.

He had already proven this point in the original Andrews and Clark operation when he streamlined the making of barrels and brought the delivery of crude to trains and ships under the company's control at considerable savings.

When John D. entered in the oil business, there were four refinery areas in the United States: Pittsburgh, which had close proximity to the oil fields as well as to coal areas that fueled its refineries; the Oil Region, which had the advantage of immediate access to the crude oil; New York, which benefited from direct access to the export market and transatlantic ships; and, finally, Cleveland, which controlled the western markets but suffered from its distance from the oil fields as well as from its greater distance from New York and the export trade.

Cleveland had a greater dependency on the railroads than any of its competitors, and therefore the costs of transportation were a threatening factor in the price of its kerosene. John D. visited all the refinery areas and again interviewed everyone in the oil business who would talk to him. Meanwhile, he was formulating his plan for overcoming Cleveland's disadvantages as a refining center and for bringing some control over the factors that put his company at the mercy of others.

Sending his brother William to New York in 1866 was an important first step. John D. was one of the first refiners to sense a shift in the kerosene market from domestic users to overseas buyers. In 1865, less than half the American product went abroad, although a higher percentage of Cleveland's output had been exported for several years. In 1866, as much as seventy percent of United States kerosene was shipped out.

With William on the spot in New York, John D. got daily–sometimes hourly–telegraph reports on prices and market conditions. William not only kept the company in the thick of the export action, but he also saved John D. the stiff broker's fees that other refiners were paying to sell their kerosene abroad.

To deal with the wildly fluctuating price of crude oil, John D. hired Andrews' brother and stationed him in the Oil Region to buy crude. When prices plummeted, Andrews alerted Cleveland hourly by telegraph and moved into negotiations. John D. made the rounds of the banks and financial community, borrowing the money to make enormous purchases of cheap crude, which he could store in his warehouses for future use.

Although the policy was daring and risky, he believed always that it was a key to the company's success. Years later, he wrote to the executive committee of the Standard Oil Company, "We must try and not lose our nerve when the market gets to the bottom as some people almost always do." He thought it a great mistake not to buy in quantity when others were frightened out of the market by depression or oversupply.

The problem of transportation costs–so crucial to a Cleveland-based refinery–was tougher. John D. knew from his commission-house days that the railroads, despite their public service franchise, would negotiate prices for favored customers. And he knew that the railroads were being hurt by the inconsistent volume of traffic from the oil industry. He began to see that he might solve his problem by addressing theirs. If he could guarantee the railroads a certain amount of business spread out evenly over a year's time, the railroads might be willing to give him a break on the per barrel cost of shipping crude and kerosene.

John D. by now had a new partner with whom to discuss such ideas. In 1867, he had taken into the firm a business associate who was to become as close a friend as he would ever have. Henry M. Flagler was a handsome, independent man nine years John D.'s senior. He had first met John D. when both were in the commission-house business and Flagler was looking for warehouse space.

Flagler, who had already made and lost a fortune, had come to Cleveland to start over in the grain business. There he met and married the daughter of a whiskey tycoon, Stephen V. Harkness. Because of his marriage, Flagler was able to bring $90,000 of his father-in-law's fortune into Rockefeller, Andrews and Flagler, as well as $60,000 of his own money. His vitality and outgoing personality were not unlike Big Bill's. John D. quickly recognized these traits as complementary to his own more reserved nature.

John D., for all his personal reticence and reserve, was never intimidated or put off by men with more outgoing personalities. Flagler was only the first in a number of energetic and bold executives he would hire over the years. He allowed these men to use their talents without undue interference; his reward was loyalty and effective management of the company.

Flagler was different from most business associates, though: he became a true friend. "It was a friendship founded on business, which Mr. Flagler used to say was better than a business founded on friendship," John D. later wrote. "My experience leads me to agree with him."

The two men lived a few blocks from each other on Euclid Avenue and attended, with their families, the Erie Street Baptist Church on Sundays. They walked together each morning to their shared office, where their desks were back-to-back. They tried their ideas out on each other and helped each other through crises.

Flagler, with his extrovert's personality, was able to talk easily and openly with almost anybody, making him a good negotiator. John D. valued this quality in his partner, as he would later value it in many key employees. "The ability to deal with people is as purchasable a commodity as sugar or coffee, and I pay more for that ability than for any other under the sun," he is quoted as saying.

Flagler's ability to deal with people was first directed toward the railroad companies. He started with the Lake Shore Railroad. As the railroad's vice president General James Devereaux later testified before government investigators, Flagler guaranteed the line sixty carloads of oil a day in exchange for

※

"The ability to deal with people is as purchasable a commodity as sugar or coffee, and I pay more for that ability than for any other under the sun."

secret preferred rates. The official freight cost was $.42 a barrel for crude from the Oil Region to Cleveland and $2 a barrel for kerosene from Cleveland to New York.

The railroad gave Rockefeller, Andrews and Flagler a different rate–$.35 a barrel for crude into Cleveland and $1.30 a barrel for kerosene to New York. The oil company was billed at the official rate and the difference was paid back to them as a rebate.

When the other refineries discovered the rebate given their competitor, they protested. The railroads replied that they, too, could have rebates if they would guarantee comparable amounts of business, which they could not.

The advantages that Rockefeller, Andrews and Flagler had obtained for their company allowed them on January 10, 1870, to incorporate their business as a joint-stock company–a popular new form of business organization–named the Standard Oil Company. It was capitalized at $1 million and its principal shareholder was John D. His brother William, together with Flagler, Andrews, and two outside investors, all received sizable amounts of stock in the new corporation.

Creating "The Standard," as John D. always referred to his company thereafter, was an audacious move at the time. It was the worst year the oil industry had experienced in its ten-year history and raising that much money to pursue such an uncertain business was quite a feat for a thirty-year-old mogul.

It was not a good year for any segment of the American economy. The general depression frightened many captains of industry. Their anxiety inspired a scheme that would later lead to Rockefeller's being labeled by the press "the most hated man in America."

The railroad plot was essentially put together by Rockefeller, as the chief refinery representative, and several of the railroads, which were feeling hard

pressed by lagging business. Under a Pennsylvania charter that had been pushed through the state's legislature for the purpose of giving some license to the venture, a holding company, called the South Improvement Company, was formed to control the smaller corporation.

The basic idea was for the railroads to combine with the largest and most influential refineries in each of the refining areas into a cartel, or association of industrialists, that would regulate the flow of oil at rates that would benefit all parties. Although published freight rates would rise, participating refineries would get substantial rebates.

Refineries that refused to participate would be ruined. Not only would they be saddled with higher costs of transportation than the cartel members, but also their higher freight payments would be given to

Barrels of pitch are weighed and loaded into freight cars at the Standard Oil Terminal in Bayonne, New Jersey.

By the end of the 1860s, Cleveland, Ohio, was a center of the oil industry. Many of the refiners who had their picture taken together in 1869 sold out to Standard Oil in 1872.

the cartel as "drawbacks." In practice, those who refused to cooperate also could be pressured by the cartel's lowering of kerosene prices.

While John D. was not the only refiner in on the scheme, he was the only one from Cleveland and he saw this as his opportunity to eliminate his local competition. He had not only the advantage of the rebate and drawback system on his side, but he also had offered Standard stock to enough local bankers to ensure that companies that did not capitulate to him would find it very difficult to borrow capital in Cleveland–money that would be necessary to fight the cartel.

John D. Rockefeller was indeed becoming the robber baron of the oil industry. He had the railroads

paying tribute to him, and now he was about to make the other oil refiners—whether they wanted to or not—join him in controlling the whole flow of the industry.

John D., though, did not see himself in this light. He thought he was bringing rational order to a chaotic business. In one of his biographies he is quoted as saying to a friend, "I had our plan clearly in mind. I was right. I knew it as a matter of conscience. It was right between me and my God. If I had it to do tomorrow I would do it again the same way—do it a hundred times."

And, as was his usual practice, he gave more than $5,000 to charity the year he started taking over the oil industry.

Agitators at the Standard Oil Terminal in Bayonne, New Jersey.

Chapter 7

Into the
Big Time

*J*ohn D. made many trips to New York during the winter of 1871 to confer with the railroad tycoons about the South Improvement Company and its mission. He met with William H. Vanderbilt and Jay Gould, railroad magnates of already legendary power and wealth, men who held no awe for John D.

Their meetings were secret; it was agreed that all dealings of the holding company would be kept quiet. An oath was drafted that prospective participants would have to sign before they were told any of the particulars of the plan. The oath began:

"I, _____, do solemnly promise upon my faith and honor as a gentleman that I will keep secret all transactions I may have with the corporation known as the South Improvement Company; that should I fail to keep any bargains with the said company, all the preliminary conversations shall be kept strictly private."

John D., William Rockefeller, and Flagler had more shares in the cartel than any other single company or person, although they were not the only oil refiners in the group. Each of the oil-refining regions was represented. The railroads saw the cartel as a way of maintaining a constant flow of traffic on their shaky lines during a bad economic period. The other oil refiners welcomed an opportunity to get an advantage over their rivals in freight costs. To John D. it was a chance to consolidate the Cleveland refining business into Standard Oil, while maintaining a necessary advantage for Cleveland with the railroads.

John D. wasted no time in implementing the South Improvement Company franchise. He started calling on his largest competitors first. Patiently and courteously, he would explain to the rival owner how the plan might benefit him. If the owner expressed reluctance to fold his business into Standard Oil in exchange for stock, John D. would carefully and unemotionally go over the alternative, which was essentially equal to bankruptcy.

He called on Isaac L. Hewitt, his former commission-house boss who had once hesitated to give him a raise. Hewitt was now a partner in a large Cleveland refinery. He hesitated again, this time in selling out to John D. The former clerk was as persuasive as he could be, but the older man still held out. Finally, in exasperation, John D. cried out, "I have ways of making money that you know nothing of."

John D.'s youngest brother, Frank, was a partner in another competing refinery. John D. told him that the Standard had a combination with the railroads that gave the company a deciding advantage. He also told Frank that the Standard was going to buy out all the refineries in Cleveland. "We will give everyone a chance to come in," he said. But he also added a warning: "Those who refuse will be crushed. If you don't sell your property to us, it will be valueless."

Frank, the Civil War hero, refused to sell out to his oldest brother and his business was ruined. He never forgave John D. and publicly testified against his sibling more than once. Nevertheless, John D. bailed him out of bad business deals many times and supported his family. Frank's bitterness was so long-lived that many years later he moved his children's bodies out of the family burial plot in Cleveland.

As discreet as John D. was in systematically dealing with his rivals in Cleveland, word of the South Improvement Company and its buyout threats began to leak out.

The news created anger and panic in the Oil Region, where the local paper ran a daily black-bordered box listing the names of the infamous conspirators. The name John D. Rockefeller was prominent among them. There were all-night emergency meetings in the Oil Region, torchlight protest parades, and petition signings (one contained ninety-seven pages of signatures of outrage against the cartel). Telegrams were sent to Pennsylvania legislators demanding that they revoke the charter of the South Improvement Company.

What really upset the industry was not so much the idea of an association of refiners–the producers had tried unsuccessfully to organize themselves more than once–nor even the special rebate system with the railroads. People were accustomed to breaks for big users. It was the drawbacks paid to the cartel out of the smaller refiners' high freight costs that really touched a raw nerve. It was also the cold and calculating attitude of the holding company in deciding who would and who would not be allowed to participate in the industry that aroused strong feelings among the independent refiners.

John D., whose name was new to the public, received national notoriety overnight. He was called "the Mephistopheles of the Cleveland Company," "the anaconda of Standard Oil" and "an octopus." Cettie–now the busy and conscientious mother of four daughters as well as her husband's confidant–worried that his life was in danger.

The producers and refiners in the Oil Region united briefly against a common enemy. They made vigorous and public protests to the railroads and all the railroads gave in—even the arrogant Jay Gould's Erie line. The railroad owners signed new agreements with the refineries to equalize freight charges for all parties. Pennsylvania legislators rushed through a bill revoking the South Improvement Company's charter. The oil producers formed their own association to protect local refineries and vowed not to sell crude to the Standard Oil Company.

John D. was not dismayed by the furor. He wrote to Cettie, "We will do right and not be nervous about what the papers say." He felt from the very beginning that he was bringing stability and order to a risky and disorderly business. He later explained his view to a biographer: "The Standard was an angel of mercy reaching down from the sky and saying, 'Get into the ark. Put in your old junk. We will take the risks.'"

He must truly have felt that he was on a Christian mission of charity, for he never demonstrated any remorse for what he had done. He saw himself benevolently offering to smaller, weaker companies the protection and superior management capabilities of the more successful Standard Oil Company. (He did not seem to question whether or not they wanted his protection.) He never conceded anything to the accusations of greedy self-interest and power madness hurled at him in every publication.

He made no public response to the uproar. Nor did he privately even blink. In the clear-eyed, practical vision with which he analyzed every situation, he saw that his mission had only momentarily been set back. Before the dissolution of the South Improvement Company in the wake of the scandal, John D. had, in fact, bought out all but three of his twenty-five Cleveland competitors. He rightly believed that the three he had not acquired would collapse on their own, as they later did.

Standard Oil Company had successfully taken over the Cleveland refinery business. It also commanded a fourth of the whole country's refining capacity and, in John D.'s single-minded view of things, that was only the beginning. He was going to take over the entire industry eventually, he knew. He believed he could do it, because he also believed it was for the industry's own good. He would begin again by appealing to refinery owners with calm, cool reason. (He wasn't worried about the producers because he felt they were weak.) If reason didn't work, he would simply have to wage a different kind of campaign.

Rioters at Oil Creek prevent a trainload of Standard Oil tank cars from pulling out, in 1872.

69

With several of his colleagues from the South Improvement Company, including the owners of the largest refineries in Philadelphia and Pittsburgh, John D. went to the Oil Region to discuss the possibility of burying the hatchet and forming a voluntary association of refiners. The association would be open to all this time—to deal with the problems of overproduction and cutthroat competition.

His proposal, for the most part, fell on deaf ears. Rockefeller and the Standard Oil Company were viewed with suspicion, if not outright hostility, in the Oil Region. But he found one surprising ally for this plan—an independent refiner named John Archbold. Archbold was, to his own surprise, greatly impressed with John D. in person—despite the fact that he had been a leader in mobilizing opposition to the South Improvement Company. John D. would shortly buy Archbold out in a friendly deal, and Archbold would one day head Standard Oil.

If there was to be no voluntary association of refiners, John D. realized he would have to make his own deal with the railroads that served Cleveland.

Cleveland refineries, because of their location, needed concessions to compete against refinery areas closer to the crude-oil production center and closer to the export market in New York. His monopoly in Cleveland gave John D. the clout to begin to play the railroads serving the city against one another for his business.

He wanted the same value for his kerosene in New York, although the crude oil from which it was made had to travel from the Oil Region all the way to Cleveland. Then the refined product had an even longer trip to the East Coast. Oil Region refineries got their crude by pipe direct from the wells and, obviously, the refined kerosene had a shorter trip to New York.

John D. worked out a grand scheme for Standard Oil on two fronts. First, he squeezed the railroads and finally got what he wanted. They reluctantly agreed that he would pay the same $2 a barrel to get his refined product to New York as the Oil Region refiners did, and he would also get a rebate for shipping crude to Cleveland. If one rail-

The Standard Oil Refinery in Cleveland, Ohio, had grown from the original furnaces and stills.

road would not give him these rates, he would use another one. If they got together against him, they would all lose the oil freight they counted on and he would ship through the Erie Canal.

The Oil Region was the loser in John D.'s railroad deal; because the railroads raised their rates to New York to satisfy his demands, others suffered. But John D. represented enough business to get his way.

Then he approached his old South Improvement Company partners from Pittsburgh and Philadelphia with a new idea for getting the industry together. Perhaps, he suggested, they should both come under the Standard Oil banner to get the same advantageous rail rates and to lessen marketing competition and price-cutting for kerosene.

In his most gracious and hospitable manner, he invited each refinery owner to come to Cleveland and go over the Standard Oil books before they gave him an answer. The two men did go to Cleveland and were impressed enough to sell their companies for Standard stock. However, at John D.'s suggestion, they didn't make the sales public right away. First, he wanted them to buy up their local competition.

Around the same time, John D. made a similar deal for Charles Pratt Company of New York, which also kept its new ownership quiet while it brought in other local companies. In the heart of his opposition—the Oil Region itself—he used John Archbold's company as his smoke screen to buy up other companies. Refineries that would never have knowingly sold out to Standard Oil surrendered themselves to John D.'s cover companies without a murmur.

It was like a masterful espionage campaign. All the participants telegraphed each other in code. "Doxy" was the word for Standard Oil, "druggist" meant the Philadelphia company, "doubter" was the code for refiner, and "mixer" was the clandestine term for the railroad drawbacks that had created all the public outrage earlier.

John D. masterminded and ran the whole show himself without letting any one arm of the operation know what the others were doing. He even treated his own trusted Standard Oil colleagues like potential counterspies. He would often refuse to tell them information on the grounds that if they didn't know, they couldn't betray the company. They also couldn't be held responsible for what was going on by the press or by competitors.

John D. started his campaign to consolidate the oil industry in 1872. At that time, there were 15 refineries in New York, 12 in Philadelphia, 22 in Pittsburgh, and 27 in the Oil Region. Within five years he had a virtual monopoly on all the refining areas except New York, where the holdouts–very few in number–had banded together.

By the time individuals within the industry realized what John D. was up to and tried to mobilize some resistance, it was too late. The power of the newly expanded Standard Oil Company could control legislatures and ruin individual oil refineries.

In 1880 John D. refined ninety-five percent of the oil produced in the United States. He had brought his dream of organizing the oil industry to fruition. The Standard Oil monopoly was complete. He also was well on his way to becoming the richest man in America as well as the most hated.

Rockefeller and the Standard Oil monopoly were frequently mocked by political cartoonists.

The Standard
Octopus

*T*he Standard's monopoly reached its peak in 1880. From that point on, John D. had to fight to maintain his stranglehold on the oil business in America. His obsession with keeping the industry carefully organized through the Standard Oil Company led to many of the excesses that made him–in the public eye–the most hated man in America.

It wasn't enough to own all of the refineries. The Standard began to take over the marketing of kerosene and the other by-products of petroleum which were beginning to be developed in the refining process. Lubricants for machinery, paraffin for candles and cosmetics, and petroleum jelly for medicinal use were early examples.

The Standard began dividing the country into regions and setting up affiliates to deliver Standard products to every town and city in the region. The

Standard's own horse-drawn tank cars penetrated the country and drove their independent predecessors out of business by cutting prices.

The Standard was not above bribing bookkeepers or other employees of rival firms. Nor was it above strong-arming people who bought their kerosene from independent refineries or railroads which gave favorable rates to independent refiners.

One independent whom the Standard had ruined devoted the rest of his life to hounding John D. His name was George Rice, and he was a fellow Ohioan who had a small refinery that sold kerosene in the South for many years. The Standard's marketing affiliate in the region was told to ruin him and, indeed, even though Rice lowered his price below the Standard's, no one dared buy from him because the affiliate had warned all the local kerosene dealers that the Standard would spend $10,000 to ruin any retailer who bought from Rice. The Standard also threatened the Louisville and Nashville Railroad for not charging Rice enough for a shipment of his oil.

Rice, whose business did go under, would appear wherever he thought John D. might be and rail at him, "You said you would ruin my business and you have done so. By the power of your great wealth you have ruined me."

John D. always denied having ruined Rice, but in fact the Standard had quite blatantly and purposefully put him and many others like him out of business. The public could sit back and watch captains of industry fight each other viciously without being unduly upset. When John D. took on the big oil refiners, it was viewed as a contest of equals. To the general public it made no great difference who won. But when a rich and powerful man like John D. Rockefeller was seen to take on a small, independent businessman struggling to make a living for himself and his family, the public went wild with rage. Ordinary people could empathize with George Rice and his problems.

It was Cornelius Vanderbilt, the railroad magnate, who said defiantly, "Let the public be damned!" when he was under siege from the press. John D. certainly didn't say anything so callous or foolish, but his silence was almost as bad. It was seen by the public as an ominous admission of guilt. That was how he came to be the most hated man in America—and the hate ran deep. Even the Baptist church, an early and frequent beneficiary of John D.'s wealth, was driven at one point to question the advisability of accepting his "tainted" money.

John D. didn't pay much attention to the public opinion. He continued to concentrate on his dream of completely organizing every aspect of the oil industry. That was his personal mission.

Andrew Carnegie, who did for the steel industry what John D. did for oil, taught John D. an important lesson about technology. "Pioneering don't pay," he said, and John D. understood what he meant. The Standard did not innovate, did not develop new products or methods. It let others take those risks and then, if the idea was good, moved in to take it over. The smarter innovators were protected by patents that at least forced the Standard to pay decently to buy them out.

Long-distance oil pipelines were an example. The idea of sending crude to distant refineries by pumping it through pipes instead of having to use the railroads had been in serious discussion for several years. Finally, in 1879, a well-financed group called the Tidewater Company actually started laying such a conduit.

John D. was opposed to the long-distance pipe on principle. Not only would it undercut his elaborate relationships with the railroads, it would also put his Cleveland refineries at a greater disadvantage. He used influence to stop bills in several state legislatures that would have granted rights of way to pipeline companies, but he was not successful in every state.

Laying pipelines that could move oil and gas directly and cut shipping costs increased the profits of Standard Oil.

He did everything he could to hamper the Tidewater pipeline that ran from the Oil Region to the coast. Standard agents bought up rights of way to block the pipeline, intimidated workmen, and even tried to sabotage the pipeline itself. Tidewater prevailed, and as soon as the company had proved that the technology worked, John D. managed to lure his people into it and buy it out.

The octopus arms of the Standard were attracting more and more public attention in those years. Standard executives were becoming involved in lawsuits and state investigations of business practices on a continuous basis. The company needed a structure that would keep its activities within the law without curtailing them.

John D. turned for help to a lawyer who had been impressive in opposing the Standard in the Oil Region earlier, Samuel C.T. Dodd. It was he–with John Archbold–who put together the Standard trust, a complicated maze of legal structures that allowed the monopoly to cross state lines unabated. It encompassed 40 corporations, 14 of which were wholly owned. But it defied outside analysis.

Ida Tarbell, a muckraking journalist who wrote a scathing history of Standard Oil at the turn of the century, wrote of the Trust: "You could argue its existence from its effects, but you could never prove it."

The Trust was completed in 1882, and its headquarters were established at 26 Broadway in New York City. John D. reluctantly moved his family to New York. He had three daughters–a fourth had died in infancy–and a son, John D. Rockefeller, Jr., who was the joy of his life.

Although he was probably the richest man in Cleveland at the time, John D. and Cettie had continued to live a quiet life there, one centered on the children and the Erie Street Baptist Church. They had an elegant house on Euclid Avenue, known as Cleveland's "millionaire's row," and a roomy Victorian summer house on a large property in Forest

In 1868, the Rockefellers bought a large brick house on Euclid Avenue, the most fashionable neighborhood in Cleveland, Ohio.

Hill, east of Cleveland. But their pleasures were simple family ones—picnics and swimming in the pond in summer and ice-skating and buggy rides in winter.

The Rockefellers entertained very little and when they did it was usually church-related rather than strictly social. They belonged to no clubs or social organizations and they were not patrons of the arts like many of Cleveland's upper classes. John D. liked to think of himself as a country boy in the city and his greatest relaxation was playing tag with his children or organizing them for an educational outing.

Moving to New York did not change that. He established the family in a brownstone on West Fifty-fourth Street, right off Fifth Avenue, and joined a nearby Baptist church. He was no more interested in New York society than he had been in Cleveland society. The family continued to spend summers at Forest Hill in Cleveland.

John D.'s routine in New York was little different from his routine in Cleveland. He went to his office every morning with a little red notebook full of thoughts that had occurred to him the night before. He lunched with his executive committee, a powerful and brilliant group of men whom he had made rich.

They were all millionaires by now and many had been bitter opponents of Standard Oil at one time or another in their careers. But John D. had won their loyalty, however, and given them the freedom to organize his monopoly into an effective worldwide organization.

Business analysts looking at the history of Standard Oil see John D.'s ability to pick and keep talented executives as one of his most important assets. The men who made up the Standard Oil executive committee in the last quarter of the 19th century would successfully take his dream to "the farthest corners of the globe."

They included his brother William and his dear friend and partner Henry Flagler, who would later develop Florida's Gold Coast as a resort area, as well as John Archbold and Samuel Dodd who had fought him in the Oil Region but joined him for the bigger battles. Oliver Payne was treasurer of the Standard, and Payne's father was an Ohio politician who would join with John D.'s high-school friend Mark Hanna to protect big business in the United States Congress.

Another was Henry H. Rogers, known as "Hell Hound" on Wall Street, where he was a shrewd private investor. The oldest member of the group was Charles Pratt, the New York refinery owner who had helped expedite the original Standard monopoly by bringing in the biggest New York refineries.

"Find the man who can do the particular thing you want done and then leave him to do it unhampered," John D. used to say. And he was quite skilled in letting talented executives use their powers without losing their loyalty or their respect. They allowed Rockefeller to continue to expand the Trust in the United States and abroad and prepare it to take advantage of a technological revolution that none of them could have foreseen at the time.

Many factors threatened the oil industry toward the end of the century. Domestically, there was the question of how long the supply from the Oil Region would last. Then oil was discovered near Lima, Ohio, in 1885. It smelled of sulphur, but John D. was there to buy up the supply because he was sure chemists would find a way to refine it. He had to put up $3 million of his own money to convince his own Standard associates, but he was eventually proven right.

Overseas the Standard monopoly was threatened by the development of the Baku oil fields in Russia, which began supplying Europe in the late 1880s. From the beginning American oil producers had exported more than half their product. The Russian entrance into the business meant now markets

❋

"Find the man who can do the particular thing you want done and then leave him to do it unhampered."

83

The Standard Octopus

Ida Tarbell wrote "History of the Standard Oil Company," which appeared in McClure's *magazine in installments in 1903.*

had to be opened up in Asia, Africa, and South America.

The electric light bulb was an even bigger threat to the industry as a whole. None of the by-products of petroleum were nearly as important economically as kerosene for lamps. Only a seer—or the visionary John D.—could have imagined when Standard Oil became a Trust that another use for their product would be established. The experimental vehicles propelled by the internal combustion engine being put together by Benz and Daimler in Germany would create an insatiable new market for petroleum.

As optimistic as John D. always was about his industry, even he could not predict the boom in oil that would persist into the 21st century. After his official retirement from Standard Oil in 1911, this boom would increase his fortune through dividends and appreciation beyond his wildest dreams. He became America's first billionaire.

John D. had put together an industrial giant that was ready to take on technological change, challenges from the government, and world competition. He himself had to live with public hatred and outrage.

In 1901, he began to suffer from a disease of the nervous system. This disease caused all the hair on his body to fall out. He brazened it out for a time, but finally agreed to wear a series of wigs of different lengths and so it would appear that his hair was growing normally.

The following year Ida Tarbell's *History of the Standard Oil Company* began appearing in installments in *McClure's* magazine. It was an astonishing journalistic job of investigative reporting on an organization that had made privacy and secrecy an operating policy. It caused a sensation and made a best seller of the book that followed.

Tarbell's book only fanned the fuels of public hatred for John D. He slept with a gun, and the pastor of his church used Pinkerton men to guard him at Sunday services. But John D. took solace with the family that he cherished and with some bold ideas about what he could do with his money.

The Rockefeller Institute for Medical Research, now Rockefeller University, which opened in 1901, was one of Rockefeller's first philanthropies.

Chapter 9

An Investment in Good Works

*J*ohn D. did not start giving his money away because the newspapers painted him, in words and cartoons, as a greedy, rapacious monster. He had, since the days he hoed potatoes for a neighboring farmer, given a part of his income to the church or some other charity.

Tithing–or giving ten percent of his income to worthy causes–was a lifelong habit. But in the years during which his greatest energies went into building the Standard Oil monopoly, he simply responded to requests that he felt were worthy and reasonable and took no philanthropic initiatives of his own. He had, for example, given $5,000 to an Atlanta seminary for black women in 1884 at his wife's suggestion. It was later renamed Spelman College in honor of her abolitionist parents.

Early in his career he had asked the Baptist church board to screen for him any church-related appeals for money. It was this group that approached John D. to help them start a Baptist college in 1887. After some internal dispute about location, the powers of the church decided it was in their best interests to resuscitate a small seminary in Chicago that had fallen on hard times.

The school had been founded in 1856 by the golden-tongued Stephen Douglas, who had taken on Abraham Lincoln in the famous pre-Civil War debates. John D. started with a donation of $600,000 in 1887 and a good deal of interest in the project. And thus the University of Chicago was founded.

By 1910 John D. had given as much as $45 million to the institution. He always referred to it as "the best investment I ever made."

It was during his negotiations with the Baptist board that Rockefeller first met the man who would become his alter ego in philanthropy. His name was Frederick T. Gates. He looked like a flamboyant stage actor with his chiseled profile and shocks of thick wavy hair. A native New Yorker, he was the son of a preacher and had become a Baptist minister himself.

After brief stints in a bank and a dry-goods store, young Gates had enrolled at the Rochester Theological Seminary. His first ministry was in Minneapolis, where he was befriended by George A. Pillsbury, the founder of the flour fortune. Pillsbury, who was terminally ill, liked the young minister's enthusiasm for life as well as his sharp mind. He enlisted Gates' aid in drawing up his will. Pillsbury wanted to bequeath his fortune to provide lasting benefit to his community. Gates helped him do it.

Gates liked this philanthropic work and began to get a feel for the challenging responsibilities it represented. It was this interest which brought him to the Baptist board.

An associate of John D. and Gates later described this strange philanthropic team:

"One would have to search over wide areas to find two men who were so completely different in temperament. Mr. Gates was a vivid, outspoken, self-revealing personality who brought an immense gusto to his work; Mr. Rockefeller was quiet, cool, taciturn about his thoughts and purposes, almost stoic in his repression. Mr. Gates had an eloquence which could be passionate when he was aroused; Mr. Rockefeller, when he spoke at all, spoke in a slow, measured fashion, lucidly and penetratingly, but without raising his voice and without gestures."

John D. asked Gates to come to work for him in 1891. The minister was given a small office at 26 Broadway, along with all the appeals for money addressed to John D.–enough to fill a bushel basket a day. Gates was not afraid to think big about how John D. might spend his money, but he was shrewd enough to know that he must prove himself first.

He did that by taking over John D.'s personal investment portfolio, which was in some confusion. All the problems of the Standard had left John D. little time to follow up on the projects he had put money into on the advice of church friends or other people he liked and trusted. Many of these businesses needed serious attention from a knowledgeable management point of view.

Gates investigated each investment, just as he investigated each appeal for charitable help. He then presented John D. with short, pithy summaries of the situation and his recommendations for action. These brief but meaty notes set a standard for Rockefeller family business communication for many years to come.

Gates also managed to negotiate a very favorable deal for an investment John D. had made in the Mesabi ore deposits in Minnesota. It brought Gates head-to-head with both Andrew Carnegie and the fearsome J.P. Morgan, who was no friend of John D.'s. Gates won John D.'s complete trust by his skillful navigation through these very choppy waters.

Gates now felt free to share his dream of great charitable trusts with John D. He felt that together they could create corporate philanthropies that would make sense out of giving, the way the Standard had made sense out of the oil business. He saw these philanthropies as self-perpetuating institutions that would advance civilization.

Gates urged John D. to apply his organizational genius to his philanthropic work. He would warn his mentor and boss, "Your fortune is rolling up, rolling up like an avalanche! You must distribute it faster than it grows! If you do not, it will crush you, and your children, and your children's children."

John D. did not disagree. He wanted to follow, in his own way, the "scientific giving" advocated by steel magnate Andrew Carnegie in his essay called "Gospel of Wealth." Carnegie believed that men who could accumulate wealth could best administer that wealth for the public good. John D. once had told an interviewer that God had given him the power to make money and that he saw his duty as using that power for the good of humanity.

Gates' first proposal for John D. was the creation in the United States of a medical research facility similar to the Pasteur Institute in Paris. Gates, inspired by Dr. William Osler's *Principles and Practice of Medicine,* wanted to mobilize American doctors and scientists in a war on infectious diseases. Such diseases as typhoid fever, diphtheria, pneumonia, and tuberculosis had ravaged the American population without any known remedies or cures.

The Rockefeller Institute for Medical Research was started in 1901 with Dr. Simon Flexner as its head. (It is now Rockefeller University.) It was the first such laboratory in the United States, and within four years Dr. Flexner had developed a serum for treating meningitis.

Gates next turned to education. He convinced John D. that a cooperative effort with other philanthropies could be much more effective in bringing change. The General Education Board, which had Andrew Carnegie as a trustee and joint programs with the Peabody and Slater funds, took on education of blacks in the South—which continued to be a concern of John D.'s wife—as its first project in 1903.

The General Education Board soon broadened its range of activity to the whole country. One of its most remarkable successes was the reform and standardization of professional medical education in the United States. Based on a study commissioned by the Carnegie Foundation and written by Flexner's brother, Abraham, the program offered financial support to institutions willing to put its recommendations into practice.

Less than twenty-four colleges and universities applied, but those that did included Johns Hopkins, Yale, Harvard, Columbia, and the University of Chicago. Their medical schools are still considered to be the best in the United States.

John D. approved, but did not participate in these early projects in medicine. For one thing, to Gates' chagrin, he kept as his personal physician an aging practitioner of homeopathy. Homeopathy is a system of medical treatment in which disease is cured with minute amounts of the substance that caused the illness. The medical establishment put homeopathy in the same category with faith healing and spiritualism.

What did excite John D. was a project that promised to wipe out a medical scourge with existing knowledge. A U.S. Public Health physician, Dr. Charles Stiles, convinced him that hookworm, a parasite that was common in the rural South, could be completely eliminated with education and basic sanitation methods.

John D. set up what was called the Rockefeller Sanitation Commission in 1909 and sent teams of young doctors out to prove what could be done. It was not an easy task. Although in many rural counties of North Carolina and Virginia, for example, as many as ninety percent of the children tested in the schools were infected by the parasite. Yet the

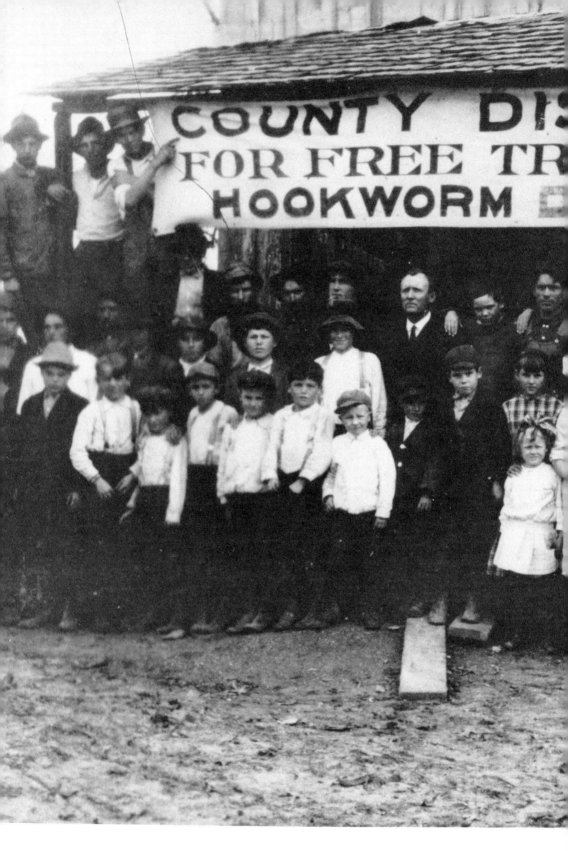

A dispensary where Rockefeller Sanitation Commission doctors worked to educate people about the existence of hookworm parasites.

local adults believed hookworm to be a myth. They believed that the lethargy, retardation, and stunted growth that resulted from the parasite were nothing more than laziness and poor genes.

Since hookworms entered the human body through bare feet walking on infected soil, Southerners said the whole program was a Rockefeller plot to sell shoes. John D.'s teams of doctors realized that simply treating victims of the parasite would get them nowhere because the patients would simply become reinfected.

The teams of doctors had an education problem on their hands, and they used microscopes to solve it. People were thrilled to look through the lens; once they had seen the worms, they then believed they really existed. The Sanitation Commission team worked with local officials as much as possible and stayed in the background. They not only got rid of hookworm, but they laid the framework for the state public health services which eventually came into being.

Ultimately, the Sanitation Commission work, supported by John D.'s money, was to wipe out hookworm in fifty-two countries around the world.

Gates finally brought John D. around to his dream—a well-endowed foundation that would be administered as professionally as a corporation by far-sighted trustees and executives who would understand its commitment "to promote the well-being of mankind throughout the world."

The trustees first tried to have the Rockefeller Foundation chartered by the federal government, but controversy over the Standard made that politically impossible in 1910.

John D. was not discouraged. In 1913 the Rockefeller Foundation was chartered by New York State. During his lifetime, John D. gave his charitable institution a total of $182,851,481. Much of this money was in stock, which the trustees were free to trade as they saw fit.

In its first fifty years the foundation granted $152 million in the field of medicine and public health, $123 million to scientific research, $60 million for control of endemic diseases, $161 million to the humanities and social sciences, $49 million for agricultural research worldwide, $98 million for miscellaneous purposes, and $61 million for scholarships and fellowships.

The visible activities of the foundation did soften the public view of John D. in his later years, and he was grateful for that. He was proud of its work and of its organization.

The Rockefeller Foundation, in fact, became more of a monument to John D.'s extraordinary career than the Standard, which provided the money to make the foundation possible. Certainly the foundation, and not the Standard, offered an important legacy and responsibility for John D.'s children and grandchildren.

Gates saw to it that the later generations of Rockefellers would not be crushed by the avalanche of John D.'s fortune. Instead, they became a dynasty of public servants.

John D. Rockefeller, Sr., in 1931 with his great-grandchildren John and Elizabeth.

Chapter 10

The Making of a Dynasty

*T*he John D. Rockefeller that his family knew was neither the single-minded tactician of the Standard Oil monopoly nor the cool, patient negotiator of better deals with the railroads. He was a pious and loving parent with a whimsical sense of humor and a great appetite for outdoor sports and games.

His own children—Bessie, who was born in 1866; Alta, born in 1871; Edith, born in 1872; and John D., Jr., born in 1874—grew up oblivious to the fact that their father was the richest man in Cleveland. He and Cettie made sure of that. Morning started with prayers and Bible readings, and those children who were late were fined for it. John D., Jr., was in charge of that bookkeeping.

Each child had chores to do and received a small allowance. There were opportunities to make more money by weeding the garden or swatting flies. All these transactions were recorded in personal ledgers that carefully listed expenditures as well. The children were also expected to save a part of their allowances and earnings and to give a part to charity or the church.

John D. loved to reward his children with shiny coins. Perhaps this was because his own happiest memories of Big Bill were his father's infrequent homecomings bearing gold pieces for John D. and his brothers and sisters. Nickels were his favorite denomination to give out because new ones were so big and bright.

Giving out coins was something John D. did naturally and gracefully. Years later, when Standard Oil finally hired a public-relations consultant to help repair its tarnished public image, the man encouraged John D. to give coins to the public. It was a popular gimmick, but John D. found that rolls of nickels weighed him down too much and switched to dimes because they were lighter. People cherished the dimes given them by the oil mogul as later generations would revere souvenirs from a movie star.

John D. was not stingy with his children. They lived in fine houses and had expensive toys to play with. He simply wanted to teach them the value of money and what he felt was the sinfulness of waste.

He himself was never too busy to check over accounting details that he felt were important. Early in the history of his thriving refinery business, he found the time to write to a barrel supervisor, "Last month you reported on hand 1,119 bungs [stoppers for the holes in barrels]. Ten thousand were sent you beginning this month. You have used 9,527 this month. You report 1,092 on hand. What has become of the other 500?"

John D. and Cettie were devout fundamentalist Christians. There was no smoking, no drinking of alcoholic beverages, and no profanity in their house. John D., Jr., who was known as "Junior" in the family, at the age of ten had signed a lifelong pledge never to smoke, drink, or swear. And he honored it.

The Sabbath was kept at home. This meant that Junior and his sisters couldn't do their homework on Sunday anymore than Cettie could cook. John D. kept a different set of rules for the Standard. He might keep the Sabbath at home—even giving up ice-skating—while barrels were unloaded at the refinery.

John D.'s children had a sheltered childhood. The family's social life was centered on the church, and when their father was away the children were entertained by missionary slide shows or temperance lectures.

When he was home, John D.'s greatest delight was taking the children out to Forest Hill. In winter there would be sledding or ice-skating, with a board to use in case of falling through a thin spot. In summer John D. would don a straw hat and take the children swimming. He led them in ferocious bicycle races and games of blindman's buff that often ended in a tangled heap of laughing bodies.

Big Bill would occasionally arrive without warning, and was always welcome. He brought Junior his first shotgun and taught him how to use it at Forest Hill.

John D. took the whole family on vacation trips on a private railroad car. A minister was always in attendance to make sure the family missed no Sunday services. The minister could usually be counted on to lead the family in spirited hymn singing to pass the time on long hauls. John D. would join in with his lusty baritone.

These trips gave Junior a lasting love of the natural world. He would later donate as national parks some of his favorite spots—Mount Desert Island in Maine, the redwood forests in California, and parts of the Palisades cliffs in New Jersey, the Shenandoah Valley, the Great Smoky Mountains, and the Grand Tetons.

Not unusual for his time, John D. expected his daughters to grow up and become loyal and devoted wives and mothers like their mother and their grandmother, Eliza. He drew up generous trusts for each of them. But his emotional and financial heir was always his son.

Junior was aware as a youngster that his family was wealthy, but it was sometimes hard for him to see the advantage of it. After the family moved to New York, he walked to prep school while all his friends arrived in carriages. His cousins—the children of John D.'s brother William—seemed to have more spending money than he. Yet he knew his father was more important at the Standard than theirs.

The protection and isolation of Junior's childhood finally was broken in 1892 when he entered college at Brown. His mother and grandmother worried about him there; they were afraid other boys might smoke in his room or tempt him into drinking tea and coffee or even beer.

Junior loved college life and wanted to be popular. He, who had never seen a football game, became manager of Brown's team. In spite of his "waste not, want not" ways, he won the affection of the players. He even got John D. to come to a game. His father was reluctant but, before the afternoon was out, he had come to the sidelines in his top hat and was loudly cheering on Brown.

Junior entertained his friends with hot chocolate in his rooms and, to his mother's alarm, took up ballroom dancing. Cettie warned him that his life sounded as if it were largely given over to pleasure. "Yes, it is true," he wrote her. "But you know that college years will never come again, so I am making the most of them in my own way."

He was introduced to Abby Aldrich, the daughter of Senator Nelson Aldrich of Rhode Island, and was quite taken with her. In his senior year at Brown, he gave a dance and invited Abby as his guest. Cettie disapproved and refused to come, but John D. showed up resplendent in his evening clothes to admire the couple on the dance floor.

After graduation, Junior entered the Standard just as his father had expected of him. But he didn't like it. Although he handled mainly family matters at 26 Broadway, he got a view of some of Standard's operating practices–and clearly found them distasteful.

What Junior really liked was Gates' work in philanthropy. However, when Gates made the Mesabi ore-field deal with Andrew Carnegie and J.P. Morgan, it was Junior who had to go to Morgan's office to confront him in person. He did it calmly, but firmly.

John D. was very proud of him for that. But he also saw that his son's interests were not in the intricacies of business. He slowly accepted Junior's increasing interest in philanthropy. Junior resigned from a vice-presidency at the Standard in 1910. He retained, however, a directorship in a coal-mining operation in Colorado that he had inherited from his father. It was being run in Colorado by Gate's uncle, who had earlier proved his value to the Standard in another role.

In 1913 the miners–9,000 strong–walked out in a strike, mainly over the right to organize. They set up a tent city and were promptly attacked by local militia. Blood was shed and newspaper reporters swarmed onto the scene. Management stood firm against unionization and hired scabs to work the mines, while lying about it to the press. Junior at first stood with his father and management, but as the violence increased and the weeks passed, he began to waver and question the tactics of management.

To help solve the dispute, Junior hired a Canadian industrial relations expert who was doing research at the Rockefeller Foundation. He was W.L. Mackenzie King, who later would be prime minister of Canada. King got Junior to come to Colorado and talk to the miners himself.

It was a turning point in Junior's life. He was moved by what the miners told him, and he felt they had a right to negotiate for the conditions under which they worked. He worked out a plan that the miners accepted in a secret ballot. He had defied the two most important mentors in his life–his father and Gates–on settling with the miners, but he came away convinced that the old Standard form of capitalistic paternalism was "antagonistic to democracy." He had become a union supporter and would remain so all his life.

John D., who never gave any of his employees Labor Day off, kept quiet. He certainly did not agree with his son, but he respected him.

Junior married Abby Aldrich, who refused to keep a ledger of her own expenses, but brought up their one daughter and five sons to record every penny. Abby brought art and theater and fun into Junior's life without compromising his sense of duty and service.

John D. retired to the family property at Pocantico Hills in northern Westchester County. There he took up golf and landscape gardening with a passion he had earlier reserved for business.

The estate already included a golf course for Cettie, who had taken up the game years before. John D. arranged for secret golf lessons for himself for several months before he challenged his wife to a game. She was delighted to have a companion. But she was shocked that her novice husband could beat her the first time he picked up a driver. Eventually, he confessed to the clandestine coaching.

Cettie enjoyed the quiet life in the country with John D. until her death in 1915. The years of public hatred for her husband had been difficult for her. In the city, they were under constant surveillance by the press. At the time of Cettie's death, the public was not yet forgiving enough to respect John D.'s private grief. He had to wait four months to bury his wife in the family cemetary at Forest Hill for fear of riots in Cleveland.

John D. continued to quietly manage his investments, work on his golf game, and improve the

William Gebele, Jr., receives a Rockefeller dime from the aging millionaire. In his later years, Rockefeller was known to distribute these coins to his friends.

views at Pocantico Hills. He remained devoted to his family, but allowed Junior and his sisters the freedom to lead their own lives.

Junior brought imagination and sensitivity to his philanthropic work. He conceived and helped design Rockefeller Center in New York City. Construction began in the middle of the 1930s Great Depression. Junior single-handedly financed the huge project to keep men working through the hard times. The family offices still take up three floors of 30 Rockefeller Plaza.

He built Riverside Church in New York and restored Colonial Williamsburg in Virginia. He had twenty-five acres of roof repaired at the Versailles Palace in France. He supported the work of physicians, sociologists, and physicists, and, of course, donated many of the nation's national parks. He donated the site of the United Nations headquarters in New York to the world organization. Abby helped found the Museum of Modern Art in New York.

John, Jr., continued his father's philanthropic tradition, becoming especially involved in architectural projects. He funded the restoration of Colonial Williamsburg, Virginia (above), as well as the construction of Riverside Church (right) and Rockefeller Center (top left), both in New York. He also donated the New York site for the United Nations building (bottom left).

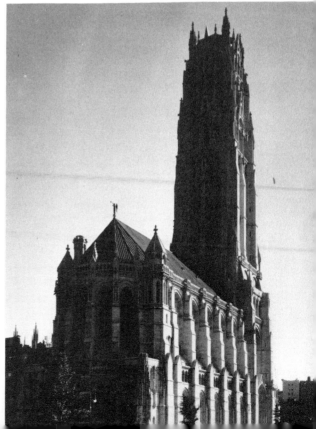

John D., Sr., with John, Jr., Abby, and their family.

Junior took pleasure in outings with his children as his father had before him, although they were more likely to be camping trips. He took the same care and devotion in teaching his family to earn and respect its money and always to save a portion and give away a portion.

John D.'s grandchildren continued to honor the family tradition of service through the foundation. Each also gave to the community in a unique way. John D. Rockefeller, III, quiet and reserved, became an expert on Asia and funded Asian-American cultural exchange programs. He also built Lincoln Center for the Performing Arts in New York City.

Nelson went into politics and was elected governor of New York three times before he was appointed vice president by President Gerald Ford.

Laurance became a conservationist and developed many Rockefeller resort areas. Winthrop served as governor of Arkansas, where he supported agricultural research and civil rights.

David, the youngest grandson, was the first in the family to earn a Ph.D., and it was from his grandfather's University of Chicago. He entered banking and became chairman of Chase Manhattan Bank, one of the largest financial institutions in the world. David's interests were global, and he became a spokesperson for American business abroad.

The only granddaughter, Abby, was as interested in art as her mother. She helped establish a folk art museum in Williamsburg, Virginia.

John D. died peacefully in 1937 at the age of 98. His great industrial creation, Standard Oil, no longer dominated the American oil business. Other people guided the corporation onto the international scene, where it remains a major player.

A more personal legacy of John D.'s extraordinary energy and organizational ability has been the Rockefeller Foundation. Structured by its founder to replenish its endowment through flexible investments, it has survived as a model for other philanthropic institutions. The Rockefeller Foundation—more than 50 years after John D.'s death—is still at the forefront of international medical and social research.

Few other robber barons of U.S. industrialization managed to perpetuate, or prolong the existence of, their good works so well. Jay Gould, for example, never involved himself in philanthropy. On the other hand, Andrew Carnegie, whose name still appears on many public libraries in the United States, set up a foundation that continues to fund educational research.

John D.'s unique legacy is the family dynasty of philanthropists and public servants he founded. The tradition of giving a part of whatever he earned to charity—a duty John D. learned from his mother as a child—lives on in the fourth generation.

Born to a wealth created by their great-grandfather, the fourth generation—men and women —were brought up keeping private expense ledgers and learning the family tradition for creative giving and public service. The family has not perpetuated John D.'s business practices. But, it has remained true to his strict private morals. There are few American families who have made as many public contributions as the Rockefellers.

Bibliography

Collier, Peter and David Horowitz. *The Rockefellers: An American Dynasty.* New York: Holt, Rinehart and Winston, 1976. (Illustrated with photographs.)

Fosdick, Raymond B. *The Story of the Rockefeller Foundation.* New York: Harper & Brothers, 1952.

Hawke, David Freeman. *John D.: The Founding Father of the Rockefellers.* New York: Harper & Row, Publishers, 1980. (Illustrated with photographs.)

Josephson, Mathew. *The Robber Barons.* New York: Harcourt, Brace and Company, 1934.

Manchester, William. *A Rockefeller Family Portrait: From John D. to Nelson.* Boston: Little, Brown and Company, 1959. (Illustrated with photographs.)

Nevins, Allan. *John D. Rockefeller: The Heroic Age of American Enterprise* (2 vols.) New York: Charles Scribner's Sons, 1940.

Rockefeller, John D. *Random Reminiscences of Men and Events.* Tarrytown, New York: Sleepy Hollow Press and Rockefeller Archive Center, 1984 (Illustrated with photographs. Originally published as a series of articles, 1908–1909.)

Shaplen, Robert. *Toward the Well-Being of Mankind, Fifty Years of the Rockefeller Foundation.* Garden City, New York: Doubleday and Company, 1964.

Tarbell, Ida. *The History of the Standard Oil Company.* Gloucester, Massachusetts: P. Smith, 1963.

Index

F

Flagler, Henry M., 58–59, 60, 66, 83
Flexner, Abraham, 91
Flexner, Dr. Simon, 90, 91
Folsom Commercial College, 18, 30
Ford, President Gerald, 106
Forest Hill, Ohio, 80, 82, 99, 102

G

Gates, Frederick T., 88, 89, 90, 94, 95, 101, 102
General Education Board, 90–91
"Gospel of Wealth", 90
Gould, Jay, 65, 68, 107
Grand Tetons (mountains), 99
Grant, Ulysses S., 40
Great Depression, 103
Great Smoky Mountains, 99

H

Handy, Truman P., 34
Hanna, Marcus Alonzo (Mark), 17, 83
Harkness, Stephen V., 58
Harvard University, 91
Hewitt, Isaac L., 22, 25, 27, 29, 30, 31, 66
Hewitt and Tuttle, 23, 25, 26, 27, 31, 34
"History of the Standard Oil Company," 84, 85
homeopathy, 91
Hudson River, 15

I

Ithaca, New York, 10

J

Johns Hopkins University, 91

K

King, William Lyon Mackenzie, 101

L

Lake Erie, 15, 16, 50
Lake Owasco, 10
Lake Shore Railroad, 59
Levingston, Margaret Allen, 13
Levingston, Dr. William (alias for William Avery Rockefeller), 12, 13
Lima Ohio, 83
Lincoln, Abraham, 88
Lincoln Center for the Performing Arts, 106
Louisville and Nashville Railroad, 76

M

McClure's Magazine, 84, 85
McKinley, William, 17
Minneapolis, Minnesota, 88
Moravia, New York, 10, 12
Morgan, J.P., 89, 101
Mount Desert Island, Maine, 99
Museum of Modern Art, 103

N

New York City, 15, 40, 53, 57, 60, 71, 72, 73, 80, 83, 103, 106

O

Ohio River, 16
Ohio-Erie Canal, 42
oil, 36, 37, 40, 41, 55, 56, 57, 83, 84
Oil Creek (Titusville), Pennsylvania, 36, 37, *38–39*, 39, 69

Oil Region, 37, 42, 50, 56, 57, 60, 67, 68, 70, 71, 72, 73, 83
Oread Collegiate Institute, 47
Osler, Dr. William, 90
Oswego Academy, 12, 16
Oswego, New York, 12

P

Palisades (cliffs), 99
Paris, France, 90
Pasteur Institute, 90
Payne, Oliver, 83
Philadelphia, Pennsylvania, 13, 71, 72, 73
Pillsbury, George A., 88
Pittsburgh, Pennsylvania, 46, 57, 70, 72, 73
Pocantico Hills, 102 , 103
Prague, Czechoslavakia, 37
Pratt, Charles, 83
Principles and Practices of Medicine, 90

R

railroads, 54
redwoods, 99
Rice, George, 76
Richford, New York, 10, *11,* 11
Riverside Church, 103, *105,* 105
"robber barons," 55
Rochester Theological Seminary, 88
Rockefeller, Abby (granddaughter), 106, *106,* 107
Rockefeller, Abby Aldrich (daughter-in-law), 100, 102, 103, 106, *106,* 107
Rockefeller, Alta (daughter), 97, 99
Rockefeller, Bessie (daughter), 97, 99
Rockefeller, David (grandson), 106, *106*
Rockefeller, Edith (daughter), 97, 99
Rockefeller, Eliza Davison (mother), 7, 9, 10, 12, 13, *19,* 19, 30, 100
Rockefeller, Francis (brother), 13
Rockefeller, Franklin (Frank, brother), 13, 41, 66–67
Rockefeller, John Davison, *6,* 6, 7, 8, 9; birth, 10, 11, 12, 13, 15;

education, 16, 17, 18; 19, 20, 21; first job, 22–23, *24,* 24, 25, 26, 27, 28, 29, 30, 31; opens Clark and Rockefeller, 33, 34, 35, 36, 40, 41, 42; enters oil business, 43; description, 45–46; marriage, 47, 48, 49, 50, 51; creation of Rockefeller and Andrews, 52, 53; 55, 56, 57, 58, 59; incorporates Standard Oil, 60, 62, 63, 65, 66, 67, 68, 69, 70, 71, 72, 73, *74,* 75, 76, 77, 80; move to NY, 82, 83, 84, 85, 87; philanthropy, 88, 89, 90, 91, 94, 95, *96,* 96, 97; on children's upbringing, 98, 99, 100, 101, 102, 103, *103,* 106, *106;* death, 107
Rockefeller, John D. Jr. (Junior, son), 80, 97, 99, 100, 101, 102, 103, 105, *106,* 106
Rockefeller, John D. III (grandson), *106,* 106
Rockefeller, Laura Celestia Spelman (Cettie, wife), 17, *44,* 44, 47, 48, 67, 68, 80, 82, 87, 91, 97, 98, 99, 100, 102
Rockefeller, Laurance (grandson), *106,* 106
Rockefeller, Lucy (sister), 10, 30
Rockefeller, Mary Ann (sister), *6,* 6, 12, 30
Rockefeller, Nelson (grandson), *106,* 106
Rockefeller, William (brother), *6,* 6, 10, 19, 29, 30, 53, 57, 60, 66, 83, 100
Rockefeller, William Avery (Big Bill, father), 8–9, 10, 11, 12, 13, 15, 16, *18,* 18, 19, 22, 29, 30, 31, 34, 37, 53, 59, 98, 99
Rockefeller, Winthrop (grandson), *106,* 106
Rockefeller and Andrews, 51, 52
Rockefeller, Andrews and Flagler, 58, ˙59, 60
Rockefeller Center, 103, *104,* 105
Rockefeller Foundation, 94–95, 101, 106, 107
Rockefeller Institute for Medical Research (Rockefeller University), *86,* 86, 90
Rockefeller Sanitation Commission, 91, 93, 94
Rockefeller University (see Rockefeller Institute for Medical Research)
Rogers, Henry H. ("Hell Hound"), 83

Acknowledgments and Credits

Frontispiece, pages 6, 11, 18, 19, 24, 31, 51, 70–71, 86, Rockefeller Archive Center.

Pages 14, 32, 38–39, 54, 62–63, 69, 84, Culver Pictures, Inc.

Pages 20–21, 42–43, 74, 78–79, Bettmann Archives.

Pages 48–49, 61, 64, Brown Brothers.